Preface

Crystal enthusiasts around the world have relied on numerous resources to ensure they were securing specific crystals tailored to their desires. These resources often contradict each other, creating confusion and often, buyer's remorse. The most common fallacies contributing to "crystal-confusion" include what each crystal is "good for", and unsound advice on how to "clear" or "program" crystals – in other words "*tell the crystal what to do."*

Here is what I know: *Working with crystals is a direct experience with energy. As humans, our energy moves from moment to moment, while a crystal's energy remains the same. This is due to its specific geometric molecular structure.*

The Intuitive Crystal Connection is a unique opportunity that invites the reader on an empowering experience of creating a visceral relationship with crystals. Through this book, you will experience first-hand the most overlooked aspect of crystals: *How the crystal system reacts with your energy.*

You will learn how to acknowledge and use your natural gifts to appreciate how crystals communicate with you. You will learn how to select them for personal use, while developing your intuition.

As a crystal lover you may have *at least* one book on stones and a few crystals in your possession. With this book in your hands, you have just found a way to deepen your relationship with crystals.

Working with crystals is a direct experience with energy. As humans, our energy moves from moment to moment, while a crystal's energy remains the same.

Crystals are more than just "pretty rocks" to wear, decorate your home, or to "feel spiritual". There is science that supports how we are influenced by crystals and a lot of misinformation about how crystals can be used, cleared and which crystals can be used for what purpose.

Science is merely scratching the surface on the vast uses and benefits of crystals. Books are both valuable resources of great information and *misinformation.*

Consider this unique experiential resource *an addition* to your current collection - one that will help you develop a visceral relationship with your crystals – beyond anything you have read before.

"Wisdom is a rumor until it lives in the body."

Like a believing a rumor about a person or believing everything you've ever read about working with tarot, you can either believe all the information you've been given OR have your own experience. Layering all the information available to you will give you a plethora of insight you would not have otherwise.

In this book, each chapter is a lesson. Each lesson builds upon the next. As you move through each lesson you can expect to hone your intuition and allow it to support how you select and use your crystals.

Assignments will be suggested after each lesson so that you effortlessly recognize and build upon your ability to communicate with your crystals. You will develop a deeper relationship with your crystals and understand how they can support you for your intentions.

During these 21 lessons, you will explore:

Lesson 1: Your Intuitive Type: *Everyone* is psychic. You will understand what your unique gifts are.

Lesson 2: Your Chakras and Your Intuitive Type: Discover how your chakras will help you intuitively communicate with your crystals.

Lesson 3: Palm Chakra Activation: Discover "**The Tools**" - a method of preparing for intuitive work. Experience the **Palm Chakra Activation** to better sense crystal energy.

Lesson 4: Taking Inventory: How Every Great Intuitive Starts a Reading: This simple trick establishes your baseline so you can easily pick up information - *immediately.*

Lesson 5: Advanced Chakra Basics: Receive a navigational tool to help you decipher what your intuition is telling you.

Lessons 6-13: Crystal Communication Sessions: You will commune with each of the 7 crystal systems. This often-overlooked component of crystal insight will enhance your relationship with crystals for heightened crystal use.

Lesson 13: Crystal Gridding: Crystal Gridding combines sacred geometry, intention, and crystals to achieve a specified outcome. These lessons offer unique insight for results-oriented crystal gridding.

Lesson 14: Crystal Space Clearing: Select the stones you'll use for space clearing, where to put them and why.

Lesson 15 – 17 Crystal Divination: Explore 3 variations on how to do a reading using crystals.

Lesson 19: Intro to Crystal Healing: Learn the primary Universal Law that supports wholeness and created an intake form.

Lesson 20: A Simple Crystal Healing Method Including placement, type of crystals & more!

Lesson 21: Recap PLUS 3 BONUS Healing and Manifesting Methods

About the author

I am an author, Holistic Intuitive, Intuitive Development Mentor and owner of Curio, Craft & Conjure – a boutique botanica in North Carolina. In each of these roles, I help people align with their intuition, power and purpose so they can help themselves and others.

My popular DailyOM course **The Art of Intuitive Tarot** has helped over 20,000 people combine their intuition with tarot to provide *spot-on* readings.

I wrote this book because, like you, I am attracted to the natural beauty and luster of crystals. After much research, I found the resources available contradicting and confusing.

My personal experiences with crystals often differed from popular belief. I learned to intentionally "tap-into" my crystals to get insight on how they will help me. When I realized my approach was unique, I wanted to offer the option for crystal lovers to create their own experience.

There is no need to rely solely on any resource, despite how popular it may be - without accessing your intuition for personal insight.

I became my own "crystal authority" and discovered that my relationship with crystals was enhanced. I invite you to do the same, by sharing the intuitive techniques I use to gain deeper insight.

In these 21 lessons, I'll help you discover why you have been drawn to crystals. I'll teach you an empowered approach to crystal communication - so you can trust your guidance and be <u>your</u> own crystal authority.

Lesson 1

Welcome and *Congratulations!*

You are about to embark on a journey that will support your relationship with both crystals and your *Self.*

First, I'd like to thank you for allowing me the honor of being your guide. You are now on the precipice of discovering just how powerful you are.

Isn't that exciting?!

Before we launch into this lesson, let's set the stage for all the lessons to come.

Let's start by explaining what this course *is not.*

This is <u>not</u> a course that peddles the character qualities and energetic definitions of a variety of crystals. There are enough resources on that. One visit to Amazon, and you will be overwhelmed with options.

This experience is going to be a very different way of learning.

As a culture, we have been taught to value information that comes from outside ourselves. This was probably because *"back in the day"* people couldn't read or write. Those who could write, would share insights and were revered as "demi-gods" – while the masses blindly memorized and followed their written words.

So – let me put this in plain English: *Many of the answers we crave, are within.*

This is an intuitive development course that uses crystals as tools for personal discovery, and (dare I say), *healing.*

This process will require you to let go of all the baggage that tells you "*you are powerless*".

You have unique intuitive gifts that we're going to identify and hone.

From there, you'll review and spend time with crystals from several *crystal systems* – to discover how they speak to you.

Finally, you will identify what crystals you want to use for specific purposes.

You can make the most of this course if you:

- **Commit to your process.**
- **Schedule the same time each day for the exercises.**
- **Gather your materials. You'll need your Crystal Communication forms printed (or a journal) by Lesson 2 and seven specified crystals by Lesson 6.**
- **Have a designated space with NO ADDITIONAL CRYSTALS, where you can sit with each of your crystals. Find a space in your home, where you can sit comfortably for up to 30 minutes. If there are crystals in the space, lovingly put them in a different part of your home until you are done with the course.**

Materials Needed

- **(Provided) Crystal Communication Forms (located in the back of the book)**: You will want to take notes after each assignment.
- **Crystals** (One for each category for a total of 7 crystals and 7 specified crystals for gridding):

Category 1: Garnet, Fluorite, Lapis lazuli, Pyrite, or Sodalite

Category 2: Calcite, Tourmaline, Emerald or Ruby

Category 3: Apophyllite, Vesuvian, Apatite, or Aquamarine

Category 4: Amethyst, Aventurine, Quartz, Calcite or Carnelian

Category 5: Aragonite, Celestite, Danburite, Iolite or Peridot

Category 6: Howlite, Kunzite, Malachite, Moonstone or Orthoclase

Category 7: Amazonite, Kyanite, Labradorite, Rhodonite or Turquoise

*Larger, natural crystals are preferred, but not required.

Gridding supplies: A larger standing quartz point and six 1" to 2" inch single terminated quartz points. (You'll want these by Lesson 13)

Ok – let's get started!

In this lesson, I want to talk about energy.

Energy is information that moves.

When it moves faster than the speed of light, it's called "tachyons". When it moves at a slower pace, it's called "quarks".

As humans there are a variety of ways we perceive "quark" energy: Our 5 senses of seeing, feeling, hearing, tasting and smelling.

Through our 6th sense, we can perceive the fast moving "tachyon" energy – which is information we sense _psychically_. We can perceive it:

- Clairvoyantly: Seeing through your "inner eyes"… often called "imagination".
- Clairaudiently: Hearing through our "inner ears"…the voice in your head.
- Clairsentiently: Sensing emotionally or physically (in our bodies) energy that cannot be seen…Like when your

friend is sad and you cry; or your wife is pregnant, and you are eating for two; or when you feel like someone is watching you, yet no one is around.
- "Spirit-Sensing": Information that is *esoterically* known or sensed. I often call these "energetic downloads", because whether I feel it, see it, hear it, or sense it – it *feels different* than the "Clairs".

We do ALL of this "clair-ing" through our chakras.

A lot of us woo-folk don't even *think* about chakras – and we should. When you understand how chakras work and why they are important in <u>every aspect</u> of our lives, (not just yoga class) - we can appreciate how they help us. We can identify how we naturally:

- Sense information psychically.
- Perceive our growth and healing opportunities.
- Attract (or repel) life's opportunities and challenges.

Crystal Communication

During this course, you are going to learn to communicate with crystals. You will sit with your crystals and use your natural intuitive gifts to understand what they are saying and how to use them. And, through experience, you will learn to trust the information you receive.

Let's be real for a moment: We have listened to others tell us what a "loving stone" rose quartz is and what a "grounding stone" black tourmaline is, but if you haven't sat with these stones yourself to get information form the "stone's mouth", you are believing a rumor.

We have been trained to honor someone else's words of wisdom while negating our personal power.

Upon completion of this course, you will:

- Understand how your intuition can support your conversation with crystals.
- Experience first-hand 7 crystals and 7 crystal systems.
- Have a better understanding of your energy body – including your chakras and energy fields.

So - before we start handling the crystals, you'll need to understand what your natural psychic gifts are.

You are now cordially invited to take the **Intuitive Type Test** on the **FREE STUFF** tab of **GinaSpriggs.Guru**. You will need the results of this test by Lesson 2 – so don't dilly-dally!

If you have taken a test like this before, please take it again. Results can change over time and exposure to new people, and places.

You'll learn why in Lesson 2.

Photo by Emily Bauman on Unsplash

Photo by Amanda Vick on Unsplash

Lesson 2

Now that you have taken the intuitive type test, grab your results so that together, we can review your gifts!

Our goal is to see where you scored highest, and how those higher scored chakra strengths support your natural psychic skills.

One of the most fascinating things about being a human being, is that we shift upon exposures to different people, places and environments. So – for example – if you know that you are an empath, and your new BFF talks to dead people, you may find yourself suddenly able to talk to dead people - while your empath friend finds themselves avoiding crowded places! This is the reason I wanted to be sure you took advantage of the **Intuitive Type Test** – even if you are an experienced psychic.

By the end of this lesson, you will have a better understanding of how your chakras help you manage, maintain, regulate, and store fast and slow-moving information.

We have already reviewed that slow-moving information is called quarks. Quarks include the chair you are sitting in, whatever device or material you are reading this with, even the sound of your own voice.

But we are now exploring tachyons, which is information that moves faster than the speed of light.

This is the information that, when doing intuitive tarot readings, helps me sense the ancestors, angels and deceased loved ones supporting my querant – *before* I even look at the cards. It also helps me sense the querants strengths and healing opportunities.

When you understand how your intuition speaks to you, it helps you better understand how to communicate with your crystals.

After taking the test, you discovered that you have one (or many!) "chakra strengths". Let's review each chakra for the purpose of understanding how each supports our intuition as it relates to crystal communication.

Have your results handy, so you can pay close attention to the specific information that pertains to you. You only need to focus on your specific high scoring chakras – but feel free to read them all, 'cuz it's good information!

- ❖ **Chakra 1** – Known for helping us ground, **Physical Intuitives** pick up sensations and/or illnesses that belong to someone else. Many Physical Intuitives are good at Psychometry - the art of touching an object and "reading" it's history. When working with crystals, you may get a physical sensation in an area of your body that relates to a specific chakra. If you know what aspect of life that chakra governs, you have specific information to work with for intuitive readings and healings.

- ❖ **Chakra 2**: Known for creative self-expression, **Emotional Intuitives** often unknowingly pick up emotions and moods from others. Emotional Intuitives are often described as "Empaths". If this is you, you will naturally be drawn to crystals that support you emotionally. Intuitively, you will have an emotional connection to your crystals.

- ❖ **Chakra 3:** Known for helping us with our personal power - **"Mental Sympathy"** carries the gift of "knowing" something for no rational reason. When connecting to your crystals, be mindful (no pun intended) of the thoughts that pop up. Your crystals will connect to you through thoughts and ideas.

- ❖ **Chakra 4**: Known for helping us be compassionate, the gift that comes with this includes **Spirit-Sensing** - channeling messages from Angels, Guides and Ascended Masters. These are the gifts that come through the heart chakra, making you a natural Healer. The spirit of your crystals will connect to you *and through you, energetically,* providing a visceral awareness of the information (energy) it is imparting.

- ❖ **Chakra 5**: Known for helping us communicate clearly, you are also able to communicate with the unseen. **Clairaudience** comes with the gift of Trans-mediumship, and Mediumship (Hearing messages from the dead). The spirit of your crystals will connect to you *and/or through you, verbally or auditorily – heard in either your inner or outer ear.*

- ❖ **Chakra 6**: This chakra is the home of visualization, helping us see the choices ahead. This is the gift of **Clairvoyance.** It is through this chakra that you tap into images, symbols, pictures or "movies" that relate to the past, present or future. Your crystals will connect to you via memories, movies, or other images that are meaningful to you.

- ❖ **Chakra 7**: The crown chakra connects you to the Divine and your purpose. As a **Prophetic Intuitive** your gifts include Spiritual Awakenings, Prophecy and Attunement to Other Worldly Entities. Your crystals will support your connection with the Divine, your own Divine Purpose and meditation.

- ❖ **Chakra 8**: Moving out of the body, about an inch above the head, we "meet" the eighth chakra. You can access past lives (through The Akashic Records) and alternate reality portals. People with this as their strongest chakra are often called ***Shamanic*** – having access to the talents, gifts and skills of all their chakras and the ability to connect with their crystals via all chakras. (That said, I would choose one way to consistently "start" your conversation with crystals.)

- ❖ **Chakra 9**: Often called the Soul Star, this chakra is located about an arm's length above the head. Through this energy center we relate to archetypes and universal symbolism when doing crystal readings, tarot card readings and clairvoyant readings. Your Crystal Communications Sessions may include Symbols, colors and signs that provide clear messages.

- ❖ **Chakra 10**: Often called the Earth Star chakra, it is located about two feet beneath our feet, and helps us breathe in elemental antioxidants and release toxic energy. The elements breathed in aid in the health of our auric and chakric systems. People with this gift can commune with nature, especially animals, trees, plants and…..(drum roll please!) CRYSTALS! You may physically feel your crystals like Physical Intuituives do, with a side order of empathy due to your relationship with the planet.

- ❖ **Chakra 11**: The energy of this chakra is condensed around the palms of our hands and soles of our feet. Many healers and shamans are known for accessing the energy available through this chakra to transmit healing properties pooled from the heart chakra, commanding the energy needed for healing. Those with this as their strongest chakra will find it easier than most to the read the energy field of crystals. (Regardless of your intuitive type, we will activate this chakra for heightened "sensing-skills" in Lesson 3.)

Intuitive Types can be broken down into four styles:

1. **Clairvoyant** – Seeing pictures, images or symbols. Accessed through the sixth chakra.
2. **Clairaudient** – Hearing words, sounds, lyrics, or guidance. Accessed through the fifth chakra.
3. **Spirit-Sensing Intuitive** – Receiving information that is esoterically known or sensed. Accessed through chakras four, seven, nine, and eleven.
4. **Clairsentient** – Being able to feel the emotions, thoughts and/or physical sensations accessed through chakras one, two, three and ten.
Reminder: *Chakra 8 gives us the talents, gifts and skills of all the chakras.*

Assignment:

Now that you have an idea of your intuitive type, take out your journal and take a moment to reflect on times you accessed fast moving energy/had a psychic experience.

The purpose of this assignment is to build your confidence so that as we move forward you don't say to yourself "*I just made that up.*"

Here's the thing: *Everything in the world, was once someone's imagination.* We have been taught to disregard it, but our imagination is the birthplace of magick and miracles.

Our intuition often feels "made up" – but the more your trust it, the more reliable the information you receive.

- Determine which chakra houses your primary gift. You will need that information in Lesson 3.

Assignment

My strongest chakras are:

1.
2.
3.

My natural psychic gifts include powers from these energy centers:

1.
2.
3.

A few examples of psychic experiences I've had in my life:

1.

2.

3.

Photo by Dani Costelo on Unsplash

Lesson 3

Each day, through each lesson, you are building up to acquiring the skills that will help you get clear information from your crystal friends.
Now that you know your Intuitive type – I want to share the value of connecting to your 11th chakras – specifically your palm chakras. In the last lesson, we reviewed how each chakra supported our ability to connect with fast moving information.

The energy of your 11th chakra – which surrounds the body and is condensed around the palms of our hands and soles of our feet – can help us access fast moving energy for heightened intuitive insight. Many energy workers are known to access this energy to transmit healing properties from the heart chakra to their clients. They can do this because their palm chakras are "activated" - meaning sensitive to fast moving information.

Activated palm chakras also help energy workers get a sense of the healing opportunities of their clients when they "scan" them. We'll learn more about "energy scanning" in Lesson 20. For now, let's activate your palm chakras!

By activating your 11th chakras, the information sensed through your palms will be fed to your dominant chakra – which you established in the last lesson – whether you are 11th chakra dominant or not.

Opening your palm chakras is easy. Before we do, I want to share a technique I call **"The Tools"** – which calls and combines three valuable energies – each of which are aspects of you:

1. Your energy
2. Divine energy
3. Earth energy

I suggest starting all intuitive work with **The Tools**.

The Tools

1. Find a comfortable place to sit for 10 minutes. Start by taking a few deep breaths, then closing your eyes. Invite your guides, angels and energies who love you unconditionally to stand in the four corners of your space.
2. Imagine your own personal sun, shining brightly over your head – with your name written on it in neon pink.
3. Above your sun is a disco ball with shiny magnets instead of mirrors. Imagine the disco ball starts to spin. As it spins it calls your energy back from wherever it may be – past, present and future.
4. Imagine your golden, honey-like energy, slapping on to your disco ball and dripping into your sun - where it is boiled clean.
5. Next, imagine your personal sun having a trap door, which opens releasing your golden energy into your crown chakra. Imagine this energy dropping down to your feet and quickly filling up your body.
6. Now – imagine your sun and disco ball passing through your ceiling and flying up and out of this stratosphere. Imagine they fly through the star-filled milky way tunnel, meeting the Divine at the end. Imagine that once in front of this powerful presence, your sun and disco ball

burst into a billion purple-light and silver-light particles and fly back through time and space – finding you where you sit.
7. Breathe in this brilliant Divine energy through your crown chakra, nose, and heart. Imagine the co-mingling of your honey-like energy with the Divine Light energy.
8. Next, imagine that a spark of this light glows in your heart space, forming a flame that now drops down your spine, through the floor where you sit, and into the earth.
9. Imagine that your Divine Flame reaches the Earth's core, planting itself into the ground. Once here, take a deep breath releasing any energetic toxins, and breathing in fortifying energetic antioxidants.
10. Now bring your awareness back into your space and set the intention to open your palm chakras.

Palm Chakra Activation

1. Initiate the palm chakra activation by blowing your intention into your hands. Next clap your hands or rub them together. Follow this up with a quick, vigorous flick of your wrists.
2. Next, close your eyes. Place your palms, in front of you, facing each other - about 3 inches apart.

3. Feel, sense or imagine petals of a flower opening, releasing a ball of energy between your hands.
4. While imagining this ball of energy between your palms, eyes still closed, move your right hand from side to side while keeping your left hand still. Get a sense of how you feel your own energy emanating from your right hand. Is it hot? Cold? There isn't just "one way" to sense it, but with practice you *will* sense it. (For example, for me, the sensation reminds me of the feeling of two energetically aligned magnets, that naturally repel each other.)
5. When you can sense the energy between your palms, that is a clear indication that your palm chakras are activated. Congratulations!
6. Next – with your next deep breath, set the intention that information received by your palm chakras be directed to your dominant chakra for discernment. Imagine the energy trail your crystal communications will take, from you're the palm of your hand to your dominant chakra.
7. When done, take a final deep breath, then slowly bring your awareness back to the present.
8. Thank your invisible team for their support.

Assignment:

Practice catching and throwing energy from your palm chakras. The more you do the above activities, the more sensitive you will be to crystal energies. Do the above activities at least one more time before the Lesson 4.

Extra Credit: Try moving your right hand farther away to see how far you can go before you start to lose the sensation.

Remember - this is not a race...have fun with it!

Lesson 4:

Let's go a little deeper on the topic of "energy" to support your relationship with crystals.
We have already established that there is fast moving energy (tachyons) and slow-moving energy (quarks). All matter vibrates at varying *vibrational frequencies*.
Frequency is determined by how "frequent" an energy wave comes by, telling us how much energy (or information) is being conveyed.

As human beings, *we are a collection of frequencies*. Our heart has one frequency, our brains another, our liver yet another. And this is just our *physical bodies.* When you add our *energy* bodies (including our chakras and auric field) – we bring in the aspects of us that cannot be measured but is validated scientifically.

Crystals, however, have a single *dominant frequency*. The definition of a crystal is: *A solid (mass) whose molecules (or atoms) are arranged in an orderly, geometrically repeating pattern.*

The orderly pattern of atoms makes crystals a stable energy body, one which, as humans - we naturally entrain with. (You may know from living with a group of women of child-bearing age, that their menstrual cycles follow the woman who has the dominant energy. *That*'s entrainment for you.)

Numerous books offer ways to cleanse, clear and program crystals – as if we "humans" influence them. The reality is that *crystals influence us*. Therefore, we want to learn how to *communicate with crystals*. They will inform us how to use them. Notice I said communicate, not "tell it what to do". A vital part of communication is *listening.* We'll be doing a lot of *crystal-listening* throughout this course.

In terms of "clearing your crystals", its dominant energetic structure doesn't allow them to catch all the cooties that people think they do. Putting your crystals in the moon or sun for ritualistic purposes is fine - but I think of my crystals as "my babies", so I wouldn't leave them out in the sun all day or let them hang out all night! I lean towards logic here: Crystals come from the earth. When I clear my crystals, I simply place them in a pot of dirt I have designated for crystal clearing. In this regard, clear your crystals in a way that feels right for you.

Take into consideration that, even though a rose quartz may have a frequency of "love", or a tiger eye may have "grounding properties" – there are numerous variables that will influence how crystals support us:

- The specific molecular composition (or crystal system)
- Color
- Size
- Thickness
- Where it is from
- You – with your specific opportunities.

Because of this, the "way" a person is influenced by crystals will vary. *No single book can tell you how you will be influenced by your crystals.* That can only be discovered once you have experienced repeated Crystal Communication Sessions.

Setting the Stage for Crystal Communication: Assignment

When I teach my students to develop their intuition, the first thing I share with them is a basic approach of establishing a baseline. I call it **"Taking Inventory"**.

Whether you are reading tarot cards, talking to crystals or just straight up "tapping-in" to someone without tools, you first want to know which energy is yours.

The process of **Taking Inventory** is simple:
- The first time you do this exercise, I suggest sitting quietly in an area you won't be disturbed, with your eyes closed. Take a deep breath, giving yourself permission to recall everything you sense when done.
- **Feel into your physical body**. What do you feel in your body? Are you hungry? Do you have any pains? Is there ringing in your ears? Simply note what you are noticing physically - without judgment.
- **Shift your attention to how you are feeling emotionally**. You may be feeling anxious about tomorrow, happy about your haircut, sad about leaving someplace, content with your life, angry at your kids or all the above. Again, don't judge it. Just acknowledge it.
- Next, **get a sense of the thoughts running through your head**. Your eyes should still be closed. You may be thinking about your "to-do" list, or something someone said yesterday. Again, no judgement – just acknowledgement.

- Finally, **get a sense if there are any *invisible* energies in the room.** This could feel like you are being watched, or a presence standing behind you, or the feeling of goosebumps.

Congratulations! You just experienced one of the quickest and easiest ways to establish your baseline before doing intuitive work. You are now aware of your feelings as of this moment. Anything else that you feel, sense, or imagine as you proceed with intuitive exercises is *intuituive information*. This process will become second nature the more you do it. It now takes me less than a minute to do and I do not need a quiet environment.

When we move on to the Crystal Communication Sessions in Lesson 6, you will want to feel comfortable **Taking Inventory** first, to establish your baseline.

Be sure to take the time to jot down what you felt, so that you are training yourself to remember your "before" and "after".

Assignment:
1. Before you start your day, take a moment to **Take Inventory**.
2. Write down your findings.
3. When you are aware of a new physical, emotional mental or spiritual feeling, ask yourself "is this mine?" Usually, doing this allows your spirit to drop what is not "yours".
4. Journal your findings.

Taking Inventory

Physical Feelings:
_____
_____
_____
_____

Emotions:
_____
_____
_____
_____
_____

Thoughts:
_____
_____
_____
_____
_____

Sensing the Unseen:
_____
_____
_____
_____
_____
_____
_____
_____
_____
_____

Notes:

Lesson 5

Did you notice how starting the day **Taking Inventory** helped you discern your energy from others?

In Lesson 2 we reviewed how your chakras support your intuition.

In this lesson you will be provided a link to your **Chakra Navigation Tool** (in the GinaSpriggs.Guru FREE STUFF tab) With this tool we can explore additional traditional chakra associations and correspondences, including:

- Color
- Location
- Physical Correspondences
- Emotional Correspondences
- Mental Correspondences/Beliefs
- Spiritual Correspondences

With this **Chakra Navigation Tool** as your guide, you will be able to determine *which area of your life* (or the lives of others) your crystals can support. The chart becomes your "cheat sheet" when reviewing your notes after your **Crystal Communication Sessions.** It also becomes a valuable resource as we move into the topic of **Crystal Divination** in Lesson 14.

Before you review the **Crystal Navigation Tool**, think about the following:

- Your history. Do you currently have physical symptoms that need to be addressed?
- Where is the area(s) of illness/symptom(s)
- What areas of your body is constricted or tense?
- What areas of your body are loose or rigid?
- Have you had surgery? Where are the surgery sites?

- Have you had any accidents? Where was there bodily injury?
- Do you have any missing body parts?
- Do you have any areas holding chronic issues?
- Have you experienced any type of abuse, (either self-inflicted or by another?) Which area of your body did it effect?

After answering those questions, you may have noticed that your experiences are related to a specific chakra or two. NOTE: When reviewing the chart, there are parts of the body that are not listed but are related to specific chakras. The easiest way to determine which chakra holds your growth opportunity is by location. For example, if you broke your arm, that would relate to your heart chakra.

Assignment: Simply answer the questions above and review the chart to discover your growth and healing opportunities.
Tip: *Many people learn that the chakra in need of the most healing, also supports their intuitive strength!*
While you are moving through this process of self-discovery, be easy on yourself. I don't know a soul who is perfect. We are all in need of healing of some type and need to keep in mind that our healing also supports our growth.

"Crystals are reborn star matter created and recreated by a variety of processes, each of which affect how energy is able to flow." ~ Judy Hall

Lesson 6

This definition by Judy Hall was my invitation to intuitively look deeper into crystals for myself. In my "book studies", I stumbled across something new to me. "Psychogeology" - the effect of geology on the mind, suggests that the minerals, and crystal forms in the location where you spend the most time, impact how you feel and perceive life.

That means that the rocks and crystals that naturally form where you live and work, influence how energy moves through your body. Of course, this makes sense because as humans, we entrain to the dominant energies around us.

Based on this, it is beneficial to work with locally sourced, natural crystals. I liken this to using local honey to strengthen the immune system, reducing pollen allergy symptoms. Locally mined crystals will support the user with the energy needed based on their unique needs, which may be influenced by their location.

Quick Story: When I was moving through a breast cancer experience, I intuitively gravitated toward sleeping with one of my numerous crystals that I found soothing at the time – a palm-size raw, uncut emerald. I later remembered it was locally mined - yet had not been aware of *"psychogeology"*.

When you "Take Inventory", you are *feeling into* both your physical and energetic bodies. In the last lesson we briefly talked about how our bodies are a mixture of energetic frequencies.

Our energy body – which we cannot see - extends about four to five feet away from our bodies. Science calls it our electromagnetic field, while others call it an auric field. Because these fields are invisible to the naked eye, I sense them as *higher dimensional energetic layers*. They are extensions of our chakras and us.

Locally Mined Emerald

The layers include:

- The physical layer (your body and about two inches away from your body)
- The emotional layer (about 5 inches away from your body)
- The mental layer (about 10 inches from the emotional layer)
- The spiritual body (about an arms-length away from us).

When I do intuitive tarot readings, the first thing I suggest my client do is think of one of their happiest moments. Why? Because doing this expands their energy field,

making it easier to "read". After quickly **Taking Inventory** of myself, I "tap into" in the energy of the querant.
I am keenly aware of the many layers of energetic information that is around all of us. My energy navigates its way around both "tachyons" and "quarks" for insight.

You are currently in the process of learning how to do this yourself. When we work with crystals, this process becomes the *Crystal Communication System.*

Our auric/electromagnetic fields (EMF) interact with all other magnetic fields in our environment – including crystals.

Crystals have their own energy field, which is why I suggest using natural, larger crystals for this course. The larger the crystal, the larger it's field.
In addition, when crystals have been treated, polished or manipulated in anyway, its energy has been altered. Reading the natural, raw energy of an untreated crystal is a more visceral experience *intuitively*.

Note: This does not mean that your current crystal inventory is no good! As you work with crystals and establish a solid crystal connection, you will become more sensitive to its energy – even in its polished form.

Crystal Geometry

There are seven main crystal families or "systems" that crystals are classified - plus an amorphous system.

Each family of crystals has its own unique internal signature which can be viewed under a microscope but is not necessarily visible to the naked eye. Each crystal system channels energy/information differently.
The amorphous system has no internal structure. (Examples include amber and obsidian.)

In Lesson 4 we established that crystals influence you based on many variables:

- The specific molecular structure (or crystal system)
- Through color
- Through size and thickness
- Where it is from
- Your specific opportunities or challenges.

The first crystal system we will review is Cubic (also called Isometric).

The single most reliable resource that will provide accurate information on how crystals will support you, is YOU. So, before we go into what the cubic crystal system is reputed for, you will experience the energy yourself. Keep in mind as you move through these exercises that thoughts, memories, images and/or feelings are part of your *intuitive communication* with your crystal.

Today, you start your Crystal Communication journey!

Assignment: Crystal Communication Session 1

1. First, **Take Inventory** from **Lesson 4** *without your crystal* in your meditation space.
2. Next, perform **The Tools** from **Lesson 3**
3. Rub your hands together, to wake up your palm chakras.
4. Grab your cleared crystal from Category 1 (Garnet, Fluorite, Lapis lazuli, Pyrite, or Sodalite)
5. Set your intention to communicate with your crystal. Breathe your intention into the crystal.
6. Place your crystal in front of you. Hold your left hand over it, to feel/sense/ "see" the information coming from your crystal. NOTE: Many left-handed people believe they should use their right hand for this exercise. There is data that indicates that your left hand is your "receiving" hand because it is governed by the right side of your brain - where intuition and creativity are housed. If you are left-handed, try both ways to determine which is best for you.
7. Relax. Keep your Intuitive Style in mind when doing this exercise.
8. **Take Inventory** again. Note the differences.
9. Finally, get a sense of which chakra is "speaking" to you. This is not to be confused with your dominant chakra, although it may be the same. Remember, every chakra is related to an area of your body – which can be determined by location. An ache in your

lower back would speak about your 1st chakra, lower abdomen pains (2nd chakra) an expansion or constriction in your chest (4th chakra) or throat (5th chakra), headache (6th chakra or 7th chakra). Again, you are getting a sense of anything you did not feel when you initially took inventory. Refer to your **Chakra Navigation Tool** if needed.
10. When you get information, make this statement to yourself: *"If I knew what all of this meant, what would it mean?"* Answering this simple question rewires the neuro pathways in your brain, allowing you to receive insight.
11. When done with your Crystal Communication Session, thank your crystal and document your findings on your Crystal Communication Form.

I suggest doing this exercise at least three times in a day - spending no more than 30 minutes in total on it.

Pyrite part of the Cubic Crystal System

Lesson 7

Your assignment allowed you to explore a new way to commune with your crystal. You worked with a crystal from the **cubic system**.

The cubic system is characterized by *axes* at right angles to each other. (An axis is an imaginary straight line passing through the center of a symmetrical solid.)

This system is reputed for **grounding, stabilizing and cleansing energy. It also is reputed for releasing energy and promoting creativity.**

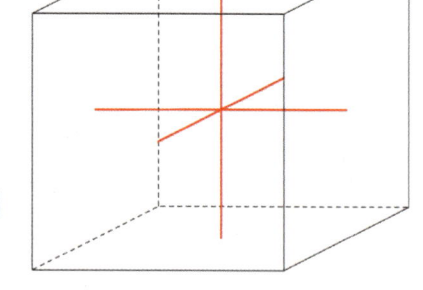

Did your Crystal Communication Sessions reflect any of the above?

If so, how?

If not, you're not "wrong". Trust your guidance! Take copious notes so you retain the overarching themes of your sessions.

As a reminder, the information you receive from your crystal is influenced by:

- The crystal system – in this case, cubic.
- The color
- The size
- The thickness
- Where it is from
- Your specific opportunities or challenges.

So – if you are doing this course with a friend, and you both are using garnet - each of you may have come up with different insight and *that is ok!*

The shapes included in this crystal system are also part of the Platonic Solids. Platonic Solids were thought to represent the five basic elements (earth, air, fire, water, and the Universe).

The cube is associated with Earth and reconnecting your energy to nature.

The octahedron is associated with air and cultivating acceptance and compassion.

Other minerals in this family include:

tetrahedron *cube* *octahedron*

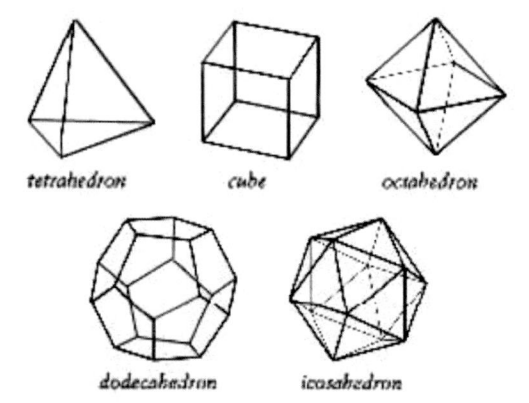

dodecahedron *icosahedron*

- Diamonds
- Spinal
- Peacock Ore
- Lazurite
- Halite (otherwise known as salt)
- AND – Silver, Gold, Copper, Nickel and Lead!

Each of these minerals have their own *reputed* energetic properties – so be mindful of what *your* connection with this system is.

For example, gold is energetically known to be "masculine" and "attract", while silver is energetically known to be "feminine" and "repel". These reputed qualities may not stand true for you – and I repeat, that's ok.

As you may have probably guessed by now, we are going to do this exercise with each crystal system over the next six lessons. Note: Each session will be different, as we are building your sensitivity.

You will be amazed at the differences you will be able to intuitively sense for each crystal system.

Let's review one of my favorite ways this information is helpful.

Crystal Gridding allows us to use crystals for personal energy clearing, energy clearing for others and environmental enhancement. It involves sacred geometry, crystal energy and your specific intention.

Sacred Geometry is often referred to as "the language of The Universe". Everything from nature, to ancient structures carry geometric forms – which, as we are aware, are a means of energy/information transmission.

A quick and easy way to "grid your space" is to place a crystal in the four corners of your bedroom, home, property and/or workspace.

But which crystals and for what purpose? Would you want the same crystal system for each of these spaces?

There are numerous books on crystal gridding, but very few take the crystal system into consideration. Instead, they focus on the reputed qualities of the crystals, shapes of the crystals and geometric shape used as the grid's base. These are also important but the crystal systems, their relationship with each other and relationship with you are *the most important aspects*.

Based on the relationship you initiated during your Crystal Communication Session, how will you use the cubic crystal system? What specific purpose(s) do you feel your crystal is good for?

If you are still unsure, let me give you a few examples:

- Did you feel/sense/imagine/recall your grandmother (or another family member else – for that matter) coming to your aid? Maybe first chakra issues around family, safety or security are the purpose of this system for you.

- Did you feel/sense/imagine/recall work issues? Perhaps a painting, photograph, movie, or book you created, saw, watched or wrote? Maybe this is a 2nd chakra opportunity around creative self-expression to address.
- Did you feel/sense/imagine/recall feeling insecure, powerless, uninformed? Perhaps your crystal/crystal system can support a 3rd chakra opportunity – which has to do with personal power, self-esteem or beliefs you are re-evaluating.
- Did you feel/sense/imagine/recall any experiences that involved anger, compassion, forgiving, or releasing? Maybe this crystal/crystal system can support a heart chakra opportunity bringing up your physical or emotional needs.
- Did you feel/sense/imagine/recall a time you needed to speak-up for yourself, make important choices or listen to what is being said to you? This crystal/crystal system may support a 5th chakra healing opportunities.
- Did you find it hard to focus? Did you feel/sense/imagine/recall someone who has a hard time with clarity? Did you project yourself into the past or future? Perhaps this crystal/crystal system will support this 6th chakra growth opportunity.

- Did you feel disconnected from God – or purposeless? Did you feel/sense/imagine/recall someone who is or has had this challenge? The crown chakra may be supported by this crystal/crystal system.

The above examples are not exhaustive – there are numerous healing opportunities that can be associated with each chakra. Refer to your Chakra Navigation tool as a guide.

The goal is that, through this process, you will be able to understand how your intuition speaks to you.

Remember this: *Intuition uses what you know.*

Don't be surprised by feelings, sensations, or memories that pop up during your sessions. THAT is your intuition. Trust it. Cross reference any physical feelings you may have experienced during your session with your Crystal Navigation Tool to narrow down how this crystal system will support you.

Assignment: Crystal Communication System Day 2

1. First, **Take Inventory** *without your crystal* in your meditation space.
2. Perform **The Tools.**
3. Get your cleared Calcite, Tourmaline, Emerald or Ruby.
4. Wake up your Palm Chakras by rubbing your hands together.
5. Set your intention to communicate with your crystal. Breathe your intention into the crystal.

6. Place your crystal in front of you. Hold your left hand over it, to feel/sense/ see the information coming from your crystal.
7. Relax. Keep your Intuitive Style in mind when doing this exercise.
8. **Take Inventory** again. Note the differences.
9. Get a sense of which chakra is "speaking" to you.
10. Spend time in your emotional field, by simply sitting with your emotions. Get a sense of anything you did not feel when you initially took inventory.
11. If needed – for clarity ask yourself: "*If I knew what all of this meant, what would it mean?*" when done with your Crystal Communication Session.
12. When done, thank your crystal.
13. Document your findings on your Crystal Communication Form.

Doing this exercise a minimum of three times in a day but spend no more than 30 minutes in total doing it.

Natural Calcite from the Hexagonal System

Lesson 8

Your homework allowed you to explore another crystal system to connect with. You worked with a crystal from the **hexagonal system**.

The hexagonal system is characterized by its three-dimensional hexagons.

This system is reputed for ***helping you accomplish your goals, efficiency, organizing and balancing energy.***

Did your Crystal Communication sessions reflect this?

Again - if not, trust your guidance! Your notes will help recall the theme of your sessions and help you determine how this system will support you.

Other hexagonal crystals include:

- Dolomite
- Quartz
- Tourmaline
- Cinnabar
- Graphite.

You may have already started feeling the difference between the isometric crystal system and the hexagonal system. You are building your sensitivity with each Crystal Communication Session.

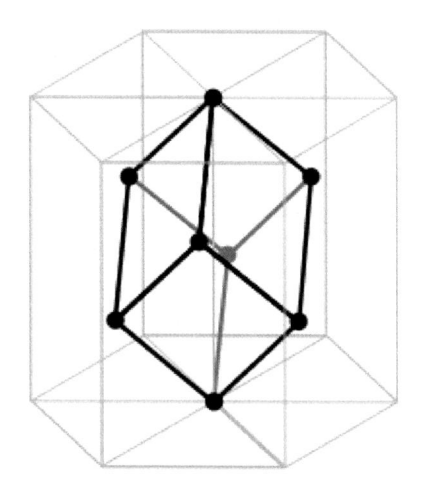

Reviewing your notes, how will you use this crystal system? What specific purpose(s) do you feel your crystal is good for?

We briefly reviewed crystal gridding in the last lesson. I have found it to be a very effective way to influence the outcomes I desire.

To the naked eye, crystal gridding appears to only influence the space it is located, but nothing could be farther than the truth. When creating a grid for personal support, like creating more love, money, or better health – *upon activation*, the grid's energy (which includes ultra-violet colors, codes, symbols, signs and sounds), transfers onto your auric field - helping you attain your desires.

> *"Crystal Gridding doesn't do the work for you; it does the work through you."* ~ Gina Spriggs

There is a constant flow of free electrons within the lattice structure of each crystal family. As we activate a crystal grid, our electromagnetic fields – particularly the powerful pattern created by heart beats and brainwaves, create a feedback loop which resonates between us, the sacred geometric pattern of the grid and the crystals. We *become* walking, talking energetic advertisements of our desires, *even when we are not thinking about them.*

Certain crystal systems *can be combined* for increased efficacy. When you include the geometric shape of the grid itself, you create a beautiful alchemical soup that will support your outcome. This is what I call magick!

After you have reviewed each crystal system, you will create a grid for a specific purpose, so take the time to think of a few things you would like universal support with.

Each assignment will continue to be slightly different so you can create your powerful yet personal process, using the crystals that feel most appropriate for your specific desire.

Now – let's get ready to review the next crystal system.

Assignment: Crystal Communication System Day 3

1. First, **Take Inventory** *without your crystal* in your meditation space.
2. Perform **The Tools.**
3. Get your cleared Apophyllite, Vesuvianite, Apatite, or Aquamarine.
4. Rub your hands together to wake up your Palm Chakras.
5. Set your intention to communicate with your crystal. Breathe your intention into the crystal.
6. Place it in your left hand. Hold your right hand over it.
7. Relax. Keep your Intuitive Style in mind when doing this exercise.
8. **Take Inventory** again, with the crystal in your left hand, about ten inches away from your body – in your mental field. Get a sense of anything you did not notice when you initially took inventory.
9. Spend time with your thoughts. What thoughts are running through your mind?
10. Ask yourself "What else?" when you think you are done.
11. When done with your session, thank your crystal and document your findings on your Crystal Communication Form.

*Do this exercise at least three times in a day but spend no more than 30 minutes in total doing it.

And DON"T forget to write down your three wishes!

Apophyllite from the Tetragonal System

Lesson 9

I hope you are finding these exercises helpful.

I'll let you in on a secret I've been keeping from you: After honoring your ability to communicate with crystals, "tapping into" people is a piece of cake!

By now you should be getting a sense of how the crystal systems feel to YOU – THE most important person on this journey.

We are just starting to scratch the surface of how you will be able to use the information you are gaining intuitively.

Your last assignment allowed you to connect with the **tetragonal crystal system.**

This system is characterized by three axes at right angles of which only the two lateral axes are equal.

This system is reputed for **protection, resolution, truth seeking, keeping secrets, adaptability and balance.**

Other Tetragonal crystals include:

- Anatase
- Chalcopyrite
- Chiolite
- Scheelite
- Wulfinite

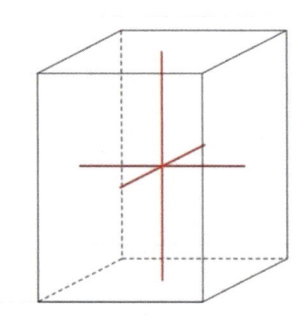

What did your Crystal Communication Session reveal for you? How would you use this crystal system?

Select one of your three wishes.

Is your wish for expansion (examples: financial, social or business?)

Is it for health? Elimination? (examples: weight or addictive habits?)

Does it relate to boundaries? (examples: protection or repelling energies?)

The energy of your intention will be supported by the crystal systems you choose to work with.

At this point, you have worked with three crystal systems. Would either of them support your intention?

If so, you may want to **gather 6 of those exact crystals** in a polished or natural state, so you can create a crystal grid. (If not, we'll continue until you discover the perfect crystal system for your use.)

The grid shape we will use is **The Flower of Life**.

This shape is believed to be the point of creation. It is purported that, after conception, upon the 8-cell stage (also known as the *morula*) this solid ball of cells not only looks similar to the flower of life, but the electric impulses of the embryo, spikes! That spike has been theorized to be the exact time of the soul's entry into the physical plane.

This shape can also be found in nature (sunflowers, dandelions and other flowers) and is believed by many cultures to be the template for everything in existence.

There are numerous shapes that are excellent for crystal gridding, however I find the flower of life to be the most versatile.

Fun Factoid: These original *morula cells* are said to remain in our bodies in the same location of our first chakra, at the base of the spine. You may recall from your Chakra Navigation Tool that this chakra is about family, safety, security and (….drumroll please….) manifesting! This is one of the chakras through which we "ground", (the other being the 10th chakra, two feet beneath our feet). When we are ungrounded it is hard to bring "thoughts" into "form" - in other words "*manifest*".

For this reason, I love The Flower of Life shape for manifesting anything from desires, to promoting knowledge, increasing self-esteem, restoring harmony, enhancing your space and even protection – given that you use the stones that feel right for your intention.

As we explore additional crystal systems and you may end up creating a crystal grid for each of your desires using other shapes as the foundation.

A very common and powerful practice in grid-creation is having a center-stone. The center stone is the point of power through which your intentions are communicated to and amplified through the geometric shape of the grid. Intuitively, I perceive our energy-body entraining to the grid upon grid-activation. Once done, we co-create with the grids support - becoming walking energy advertisements for our grids!

A **standing quartz point** plays the role of the centerstone perfectly due to its amplifying qualities. When you are looking to bring something into your world from the outside, a standing quartz point is the perfect choice.

Hot Tip: Spheres are wonderful for their ability to emit energy evenly throughout an environment, like a healing space, bedroom or living room.

There are many crystal shapes that offer different energetic qualities making them perfect for center points which we will explore in Lesson 13.

For now, you may want to secure at least one standing quartz point for personal use.

Assignment: Crystal Communication System Day 4

1. First, **Take Inventory** *without your crystal* in your meditation space.
2. Perform **The Tools.**

3. Get your cleared Amethyst, Aventurine, Quartz or Carnelian.
4. Wake up your Palm Chakras.
5. Set your intention to communicate with your crystal. Breathe your intention into the crystal.
6. Place it in your left hand. Hold your right hand over it. What do you sense?
7. Relax. Keep your Intuitive Style in mind.
8. **Take Inventory** again, now with the crystal in your left hand, about five inches away from just below your naval. Get a sense of any emotions you did not notice when you initially took inventory.
9. Spend time with your emotions. This is your emotional field. What emotions are experiencing? *Emotions and intuition are often related.*
10. Next - breath in the energy of the crystal, imagining it's message traveling to your dominant chakra, revealing the perfect insight meant just for you.
11. Ask yourself "What else?" when you think you are done.
12. When done with your session, thank your crystal and document your findings on your Crystal Communication Form.

Again, do this exercise a few times in a day but no more than 30 minutes in total.

Review your past sessions to get a sense of how much more information you are perceiving.

Also, if you haven't already done so, secure your additional crystals (6 of your favored crystal system so far, 6 1" -2" inch single terminated crystal point and a standing quartz point.)

Polished Carnelian from the Trigonal Crystal System

Lesson 10

During your assignment, you explored the **Trigonal Crystal System**. This system is characterized by three equal and equally inclined axes.

Crystals of this type are known to ***protect the environment and your aura. They also generate, store and radiate energy.***

Other Trigonal crystals include:

- Ametrine
- Agate
- Bloodstone
- Chalcedony
- Chrysoprase

- Citrine
- Hematite
- Jasper
- Rose Quartz

Note: The Trigonal system is an aspect of the hexagonal system. Under a microscope, this system features a triangular internal structure. The hexagonal system features a hexagonal internal structure – which also *includes a triangular lattice.* You'll discover many crystals represented in both categories.

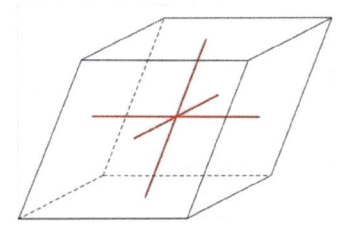

Compare your notes from this assignment to your notes from the hexagonal Crystal Communication Session. Do your notes reveal a difference, or did they "feel" similar?

Your standing quartz point, which you will use when we create your crystal grid, is in this family.

Your six 1"- 2" single terminated (featuring only one point) quartz points for will store and communicate your intention to the larger center-stone, when you make your grid. They will be *an addition* to the stones you may have already selected.

You may have recognized by now that as we move through each assignment, you are prompted to explore a different way to commune with your crystals. We started by simply sensing the energy of the crystal without holding it, and gradually moved to holding the crystals and placing them near different chakras and different energy fields.

The goal is for you to be exposed to a variety of ways to experience crystal communication so you can determine what feels most best for you. In time, you will be able to experience your crystal's energy without being anywhere near it. Just like your energetic connection to your loved ones, you are establishing an energetic connection to your crystals that will defy proximity.

Quick story: I woke up one night and could not go back to sleep. I just *thought* of my crystal that I use to relax (iolite) and before you know it, I was out like a light!

Let's move forward in our journey.

Assignment: Crystal Communication System Day 5

1. First, **Take Inventory** *without your crystal* in your meditation space.
2. Perform **The Tools.**
3. Get your cleared Aragonite, Celestite, Danburite, Iolite or Peridot.
4. Wake up your Palm Chakras. (Rub your hands together)
5. Set your intention to communicate with your crystal. Breathe this intention into the crystal.
6. Place it in your left hand. Hold your right hand over it. What do you sense?
7. Relax. Keep your Intuitive Style in mind.

8. **Take Inventory** again, now with the crystal in your left hand. Stretch your perception to your Spiritual field. Get a sense of any images or physical, emotional or spiritual energy you did not notice with your initial inventory.
9. Ask yourself: Which energy field or chakra is holding my attention?
10. Breath in the energy of the crystal, imagining it's message traveling to your dominant chakra, revealing even more information.
11. Ask yourself "What else?" when you think you are done.
12. When done with your session, thank your crystal and document your findings on your Crystal Communication Form.

Do this exercise three times in a day. In one of your sessions, revisit a crystal from a previous crystal system to note the differences. Intuitive insight becomes obvious when you sit with two different systems because you are reading two different energies, back-to-back.

As usual, spend no more than 30 minutes in total with these exercises.

Review past Crystal Communication Sessions to expand your awareness of your intuitive perspectives from lesson to lesson.

Raw Iolite from the Orthohombic Crystal System

Lesson 11

During your assignment, you communicated with the **orthorhombic crystal system.**

This system is characterized by three unequal axes at right angles.

Orthorhombic crystals are known for **cleansing, protecting and stabilizing energy.**

Other orthorhombic crystals include:

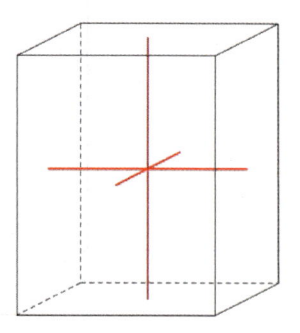

- Chrysoberyl
- Tanzanite
- Topaz
- Mordenite
- Holtite

What thoughts, memories, images, and/or feelings did you experience when you sat with your crystal?

When you review the list of crystals provided for this exercise, (Aragonite, Celestite, Danburite, Iolite and Peridot), you may notice that only one of them (peridot) is popular for "cleansing, protecting or stabilizing energy". It is this reason it is important to sit with your crystals yourself.

Shifting into The Zone

You may also have noticed by now that you have established a distinct process to access intuitive information. When teaching people how to access their intuition, I always encourage them to create an "on-switch" – very much like the character "Jeanie" in "*I Dream of Jeannie*" or "Samantha" in "*Bewitched*". Each of them had their own unique way of letting their bodies know they were accessing their personal brand of magick...using their "on-switch".

By repeating the process of **Taking Inventory**, performing **The Tools**, and simply *rubbing your hands together*, you are performing a practical ritual that not only allows you to wake up your palm chakras but also allows you to "shift" from recognizing "quark" slow-moving energy to recognizing "tachyon" energy that moves faster than the speed of light.

You will find this simple protocol helpful when you do any type of intuitive work, whether you are communicating with crystals, reading tarot cards, communing with the dead or just reading someone's energy field.

When you are in the process of creating your crystal grid, you will perform this ritual before you place the stones. You will be in "The Zone" for your entire Crystal Grid Creation process.

I am confident that by now, due to repetition, you can perform this pre-ritual quickly and easily.

Assignment: Crystal Communication System Day 6

1. First, **Take Inventory** *without your crystal* in your meditation space.
2. Perform **The Tools.**
3. Get your cleared Howlite, Kunzite, Malachite, Moonstone or Orthoclase
4. Rub your hands together.
5. Set your intention to communicate with your crystal. Breathe this intention into the crystal.
6. Place it in your right hand. Hold your left hand over it. What do you sense?
7. Relax. Keep your Intuitive Style in mind.

8. **Take Inventory** again, now with the crystal in your left hand. Hold your right hand open, comfortable in your lap.
9. Next, go deeper in your **Taking Inventory** process, actively spend time in each energy field:
    - Physical
    - Emotional
    - Mental
    - Spiritual
10. Get a sense of any new images or physical, emotional, mental or spiritual energy.
11. Ask yourself: Which energy field or chakra is holding my attention?
12. Breath in the energy of the crystal, imagining it's message traveling to your dominant chakra, revealing even more information.
13. Ask yourself "What else?" when you think you are done.

When done with your session, thank your crystal and document your findings on your Crystal Communication Form.

Do this exercise three times in a day. Revisit your crystal from a previous crystal system to note the differences in one of the sessions. Spend no more than 30 minutes in total with these exercises.

Review past Crystal Communication Sessions to continue expanding your awareness of your intuitive perspectives from lesson to lesson.

Orthoclase from the Monoclinic Crystal System

Lesson 12

During your assignment you communicated with the **monoclinic crystal system**. This system contains three vectors of unequal lengths forming a rectangular prism with a parallelogram as its base.

This system is reputed for *improving current circumstances, protection, or keeping what you already have.*

Other monoclinic crystals include:

- Kaolin
- Muscovite
- Lazulite

- Scheelite
- Diopside

What thoughts, memories, images, and/or feelings did you experience when you sat with your crystal?

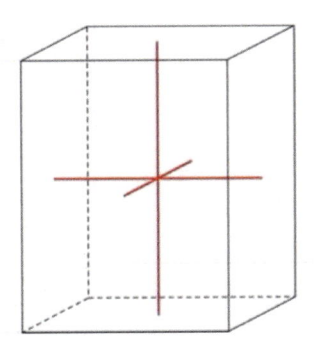

True Story: One year my daughter and I went on a buying trip to a crystal show - purchasing crystals to sell at our store. When we were about to leave, I passed a small table with the most unusual crystal. I stopped to get a closer look at this crystal and knew one thing was certain: I HAD to have it!

I found out what the stone was called (Orthoclase – I had never heard of it) but didn't understand my sense of urgency until, upon further research I learned some very interesting stuff!

Orthoclase, as you are aware, is in the monoclinic system and we've learned that this system is reputed for *"helping you keep what you already have"*. As a stone, is also reputed for *helping maintain youth*. Ironically, (or not) I purchased this stone the day before my 56th birthday!

Moral of the story: ALWAYS pay attention to your intuition. *Notice what you notice.*

This story leads me to another easy and powerful way to select crystals. Numerous crystal resources suggest "finger dowsing" or pendulum use for crystal selection.

When people walk into my store and ask: "What are the best crystals for...? (place any desire here), I recognize they are very comfortable using the "logical approach" we've all been trained to trust.

Yet I almost always suggest they look at our collection of crystals, select the crystals they are attracted to, and from there refer to one of our numerous crystal resources.

Every.Single. Time, they leave feeling confident in their choice. The difference, however, is they allowed their heart to lead them, and not their head or a perceived "authority". They allowed themselves to be an authority.

On occasion, however, someone must take their process a step further. They may be attracted to 5 crystals and only have the budget for 3, or simply feel torn. When this is the case, I suggest a technique called *applied kinesiology.*

There are many types of applied kinesiology – in fact, as far as I am concerned, using a pendulum is an aspect of it.

So, while many crystal resources suggest finger dowsing or pendulum use for crystal selection, my suggested approach combines the two.

Using Your Body as a Pendulum

Tip: Your body doesn't lie. When you use *your body* as a pendulum you can easily and quickly perceive what is in your highest good.

How it works:

1. Establish your baseline. To do this, you must know how your body says *"yes"* and how it says *"no"*. Remove your watch and hold nothing in your hands for this exercise. Stand with knees "unlocked" (if you ski, I would say use *"ski-knees"* which basically means they are a little loose, and ever so slightly bent.)

2. Say aloud: *"My name is (whatever your name is)*. Notice if your body leaned backward or forward. For some, the movement is very subtle. For others, the movement is so dramatic it knocks them over. Whichever way your body moved, that is your "Yes."

3. Next, for confirmation, you will say: *"My name is David Bowie"*. *Needless to say - this lie will inspire your body to sway in the opposite direction.* Whichever way your body moves, THAT is your "No."

4. Finally, move through this exercise with each crystal option you are presented with, looking for your body's "Yes's".

Extra credit: You can use this exercise for food, medication, and even people! ;o)

*Many people believe that *forward* movement is *"Yes"* and backward movement is *"No"*. After doing this with thousands of clients at my store, I realize that some of us are energetically different, thus the opposite is true.

Assignment: Crystal Communication System Day 7

1. First, **Take Inventory** *without your crystal* in your meditation space.
2. Perform **The Tools.**
3. Get your cleared Amazonite, Kyanite, Labradorite, Rhodonite or Turquoise
4. Rub your hands together.
5. Set your intention to communicate with your crystal. Breathe this intention into the crystal.
6. Choose any method you desire to gain insight from your crystal, whether we have it used previously, or you have come up with something on your own. What do you sense?
7. Relax. Keep your Intuitive Style in mind.
8. **Take Inventory** again.
9. Get a sense of any new images or physical, emotional, mental or spiritual energy.
10. Ask yourself: Which energy field or chakra is holding my attention?
11. Breath in the energy of the crystal, imagining it's message traveling to your dominant chakra, revealing even more information.
12. Ask yourself "What else?" when you think you are done.

When done with your session, express your gratitude and document your findings on your Crystal Communication Form.

As usual, do this exercise three times in a day, revisiting a crystal from a previous crystal system to note the differences. Spend no more than 30 minutes in total with these exercises.

Review past Crystal Communication Sessions to continue expanding your awareness of your intuitive perspectives.

Natural Labradorite from the triclinic crystal system

Lesson 13

Congratulations!

You completed your crystal communication assignments, and we'll now start to play with our crystals.

Your final Crystal Communication assignment you visited the **triclinic crystal system.**

This asymmetric system has three unequal axes intersecting at oblique angles.

It is reputed for *completion, energy integration, focus, as well as shielding from unwanted energy.*

What did your session reflect? What **thoughts, memories, images, and/or feelings** did you experience when you sat with your crystal?

Today, let's get to the meat and potatoes of this course.

To recap, by now you have:

- Established your intuitive type.
- Learned how to Take Inventory to establish a baseline for your readings.
- Learned *The Tools* to create shift you into *The Zone*.
- Communicated with each crystal system, using your natural intuitive gifts.

You have also been receiving bite size chunks of information about crystal grids and by now have already:

- Selected at least one of your 3 wishes you'll get crystal support with.
- Acquired crystals from the crystal system you feel will best support your intention(s).
- Reviewed and received the sacred **Flower of Life** shape to use as the foundation for your grid.
- Acquired a center stone – a standing crystal point (from the tetragonal system) to hold and radiate your intention to the world.
- Acquired 6 single terminated 1'-2' inch quartz crystals to communicate your intentions to the center stone.

Back in Lesson 9 we talked about other shapes that can be used as your center stone and they properties the outer shape of the crystal would add to you grid. To be clear, we have been exploring the energetic qualities of the internal lattice – which is invisible to the naked eye. The outer shape of a crystal, even when manipulated, can alter the energetic qualities of the crystal too. Here is a brief list of other shapes and how they are helpful:

Clusters: These radiate energy in multiple directions.

Eggs: The smaller end focuses energy. The larger, rounded end radiates energy more widely. The smaller end is perfect for directing energies during healing sessions while the rounded end pointed up is best for grids that radiate out.

Generators: This standing crystal features 6 planes that all meet at the tip. It is great to use as a center stone for your crystal grid intentions.

Scepter: In appearance, this looks like a crystal formed around a rod and is perfect to activate a grid because it can energetically support the restructuring or directing of power.

Square: Ground and anchor intentions. I like to use these around my grids, to anchor my intentions.

Wands: Usually long and pointed are usually used to either focus energy or bring in new energy depending on which way the point is facing. Also perfect for grid activation.

Consider This: Crystal System Combinations.

I have found that certain crystal systems support each other. For example, when I am calling in success, I prefer to use the trigonal crystal system (like citrine and carnelian) with cubic systems (like pyrite) and tetragonal crystals (like quartz). I also like to anchor my grids with a tetragonal crystal, like tiger eye.

Tip: Look at both the crystal qualities and the crystal system when selecting your crystal choices. Document your crystal choices when creating your grid so you can keep track of which combinations work best for you.

Okay! You are now ready for this next step. Please read through the following twice, then proceed with the actual activity as your assignment.

Creating Your Crystal Grid

Creating a crystal grid is not a "pray and wait" game of faith. It is an alchemical influence of Universal Energies supported by action, intention, emotion, sacred geometry and crystals.

Creating a crystal grid is like a moving prayer; each component representing a well-thought-out expression of your deepest desires.

Many people use prayer as the single vehicle towards intention. Creating a crystal grid combines the alchemical influence of your intentions, which are motivated by desire (emotion), sacred geometry, very specific energy based on the crystal system you selected, and the action of you creating and activating the grid.

Creating a crystal grid is not a "pray and wait" game of faith. It is an alchemical influence of Universal Energies supported by action, intention, emotion, sacred geometry and crystals.

I like my crystal grids to look beautiful. This is not a hard and fast rule, but your grid will be standing for at least 40 days, so you may as well enjoy looking at it. We all know that beauty is in the eye of the beholder, so give yourself permission to embellish your grid as you see fit. As you glance at your finished grid while moving through your day, you want your internal energetic response to be more along the lines of *"You go, girl!"* as opposed to *"Are you done yet?"*

Basic Steps to Creating Your Grid

1. Start by gathering your cleansed crystals you have selected based on your specific intention. Be sure you have your Flower of Life template. (Provided)
2. **Take Inventory** and perform **The Tools** in the space you are creating your grid.
3. Rub your hands together.
4. Set your intention to communicate with your crystals. Breathe this intention into your crystals.
5. **Write your intention** on a piece of paper.
6. Place your written intention under your center stone in the center of your Flower of Life.

7. Place your support crystals from the crystal system supporting your intention on the grid where it feels natural to you.
8. By now you should have 7 crystals on your grid – (6) supportive crystals and your focus crystal. Now, add your quartz points in areas that are in alignment with the support-crystals and focus crystal. They are carrying the information to the center stone, so make sure their point is facing the center of the grid, *pointing inward.*
9. Add any embellishments if you choose.
10. Activate your grid.

Grid Activation Steps

a) You may choose to use your finger or a crystal "wand" or point for this exercise. Keep in mind that quartz can amplify energy, so a quartz point may be preferred.

b) Take a deep breath. Feel, sense and imagine your desired outcome. Once you are "there", point your finger (or crystal wand) at the center stone; then, out to a line of supporting stones (at the 12:00 position), then back to the center stone, then back out to the next line of supporting stones (at the

1:00 position); almost like tracing spokes on a wheel, moving in a clockwise motion.
c) Trace back and forth around the Flower of Life a total of 3 times.
d) When done, point at the top of the center stone and affirm your intention in a positive and present tense statement. (*"I am so happy experiencing the love of my life!"* or *"I have all the resources needed to pay all my bills."*).
e) You are Done! Leave your grid up for at least 40 days.

Note: The number of crystals you use may be based on grid shape and size.

Lesson 14

"Crystals work through the transmission of energy and the adjustment of subtle vibrations" ~ Judy Hall

Who's subtle vibrations? Ours, of course!

Another beautiful way to create a grid is to create a protective energetic grid around your home.

The following exercises use the natural "template" of your environment.

Whether it is your home on private property or the apartment (or room) you rent, you can easily create an energetic protective net.

This net will support you and your loved ones from unwanted energies, inclusive of
Laser Point in Plant

electronic energies, which have been scientifically proven to weaken our auric field.

We know now from our studies that orthorhombic, monoclinic and triclinic crystal systems contain the internal geometric lattice conducive to supporting release and containing the geometric lattice that supports protective energy.

You may have read that black tourmaline is great for grounding. And by now you may also know that black tourmaline is part of the hexagonal crystal system – which supports growth and expansion.
You may even have experienced completely different insight from your Crystal Communication Session.

In general, stones that are darker contain a high content of iron. Scientists have detected an iron octahedron in the center of the Earth through sonar experiments. Because of this, metaphysicians have determined that stones with high iron content are excellent for grounding.

In addition, shungite, which is not a crystal but more of a mineral, has a high content of carbon. Shungite is believed to have the ability to completely neutralize the dangerous frequencies from EMF radiation due to the *fullerenes inside. **Fullerenes are hollow, pure carbon, molecules.**

So, in this lesson, our goal is to ground and protect your home from harmful influences using both black tourmaline and shungite. Note: If, through your Crystal Communication Sessions, there is an alternate stone you would prefer, you are free to do so.

In addition, we'll explore other unique ways to enhance the energy of your home using crystals.

Read through the following information to determine which you will do. You may need to secure additional crystals for this exercise, but the small investment is worth it.

Your Assignments:

1. Based on the information you now have available to you, gather 4 black tourmaline crystals (or your substitute) and a shungite stone for any areas you use the most (or any) electricity such as:
    - TV's
    - Computers
    - Microwaves
    - Charging stations
2. Gather your stones.
3. **Take Inventory** and perform **The Tools** in your space.
4. Rub your hands together.
5. Breathe your intention into your stones.

6. Strategically place your Black Tourmaline/or substitute in the four corners of your property, home or space. Add the shungite next to your electrical appliances.

Creating Balance in Your Space:

In this exercise you will use crystals to create balance in a living area or work area. Having crystals in your living space is an important part of becoming attuned with the frequency of the crystals. Through the process of attunement, you will begin to resonate with crystalline energies – which makes it easier to commune with them.

Additional Reasons to have a balanced living area:

- Helps you feel better.
- Helps plants grow better in the space.
- Helps your pets feel better.

What You'll Need:

- 12 single terminated quartz or citrine points of the same size and approximate weight. *Clarity is not important.
- Determine magnetic north (you can use the compass app on your cell phone).

1. **Take Inventory** and perform **The Tools** in your space.
2. Rub your hands together.
3. Breathe your intention into your crystals.

4. Place 6 crystals along the north wall or windowsill of your space, with the points facing south. (6 is the number for healing.)

5. Place 6 crystals along the east wall or windowsill with the points facing west.

Space Clearing Tips:

- NEVER place crystals around your computer, as they are *amplifiers* of energy. Electricity is not the energy you want amplified in your home.

- Do place wands or lasers point side up in a house

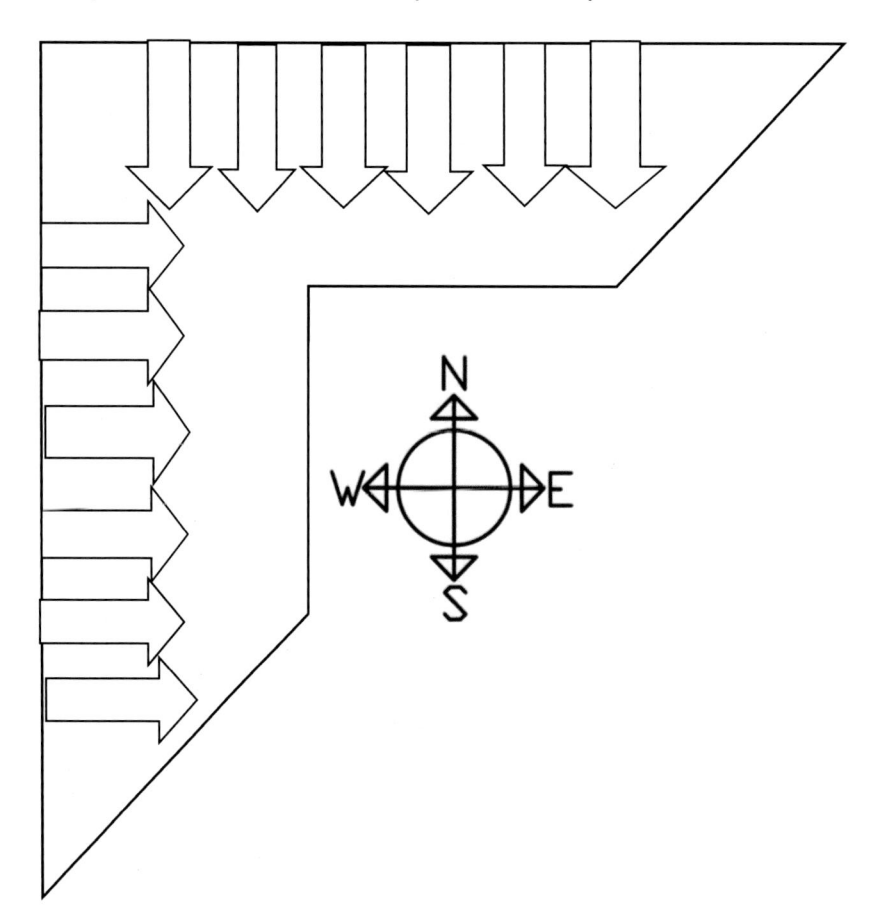

plant. This helps spread negative ions, similar to a salt lamp!

Lesson 15

Some psychic *"elitists"* believe that using tools, (like tarot cards, bones, crystals feathers, and shells) make you less of "an intuitive".
<u>Nothing can be further from the truth.</u>
Each of us draws our knowledge from books, and our wisdom from cellular memory and experience.
Truth be told, our intuition is always under the surface, waiting to reveal the unknown via signs, omens and divinatory tools.
Welcome to the Divination portion of the course!
First, let's combine the definition of "Divination" and "Crystals".
Divination: *The art or practice that seeks to discover hidden knowledge by the interpretation of omens or by the aid of tools or supernatural powers.*
Crystals: *Homogeneous, solid substances having a natural geometrically repeating form with symmetrically arranged plane faces.*
<u>**Crystal Divination**</u>: **The art of seeking hidden knowledge of the future by combining intuition, crystals and/or your chosen grid.**

"Intuition uses what you know". ~ Gina Spriggs

Clients love to be able to connect with the message you are divining from Spirit in any way, shape or form. I can tell you from personal experience that very few people can resist the luster of a beautiful crystal.
You may want to secure crystals specifically for divination. I suggest you read through this lesson to determine which divination system you will use. If you do choose to secure additional crystals specifically for divination, you will want to be intentional about size, shape, and color.

1st Technique: YES or NO Divination

A crystal can provide a "yes" or "no" answer.
You can either use a pendulum with a crystal on the end OR use a crystal that has a smooth a significant difference between one side and the other.

If using a pendulum, determine your "yes" and your "no" first.
- Create a time and space where you will have no distractions for 15 minutes.
- In a comfortable seated position, take a deep breath in through your nose, and out through your mouth three times.
- Holding your crystal pendulum in one hand, close your eyes and ask it to show you "yes".
- Next, ask your pendulum to show you "no".
- Now you are ready to ask it a "yes" or "no" question.

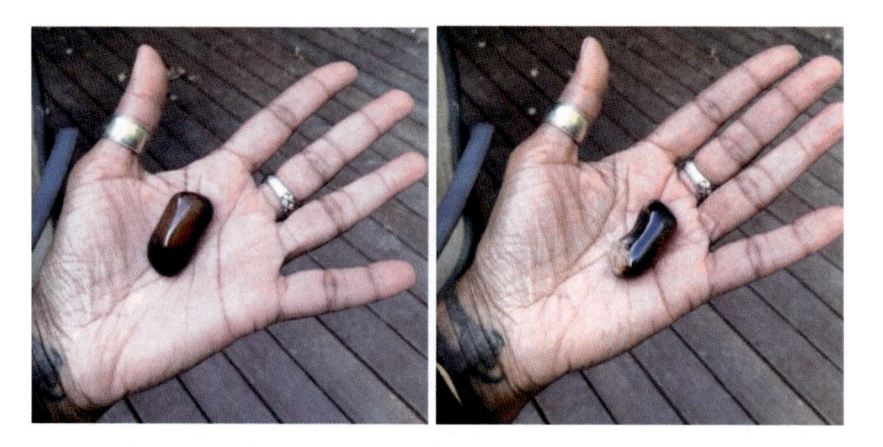

If you chose a crystal with significant differences between one side and the other, determine which is "yes" and which is "no".

From here:

1. **Take Inventory** and perform **The Tools** in your space.
2. Rub your hands together.
3. Breathe your intention into your crystal.
4. Hold your question in your mind while rolling the crystal in your palm like a coin or dice.
5. Cast your crystal, releasing it from your palm.
6. You have your answer.

This technique is so easy peasy but - I am going to be the devil's advocate, here: *If you ask yes or no questions, you will only get yes or no answers.*

My clients like "more" (so do I!), so we'll explore more other techniques, so you are able to offer a more insightful reading.

Lesson 16

Before we explore an additional divination technique, let's review the tools we have at our disposal.

We have already learned that each chakra has colors associated with them, as well as areas of life they govern.

What if we layered this knowledge with synchronicity for a more insightful reading?

To do this we would need crystals that are the colors associated with each chakra.

This list of suggested crystals is not exhaustive. Feel free to combine your current crystal inventory with your intuition to determine what crystal goes with what chakra.

*Suggested Crystals:

1. Red Jasper, Garnet or Tiger Eye for the **Root Chakra**
2. Carnelian or Orange Calcite for the **Sacral Chakra**
3. Amber or Citrine for the **Solar Plexus Chakra**
4. Green Aventurine or Rose Quartz for the **Heart Chakra**
5. Lapis or Aqua Marine for the **Throat Chakra**
6. Amethyst or Iolite for the **3rd Eye Chakra**
7. Clear Quartz for the **Crown Chakra**

When cross referencing crystal colors, crystal correspondences and with the chakra of the corresponding color you can gain deeper insight.
I suggest you have the following on hand for the following techniques:

- A minimum of 7 Crystals in any shape that are related to the 7 chakras.
- A dark bag (or box) to hold your crystals.

TIP: When we ask "should" questions, we literally toss away our power! So – for this modality, we will explore two additional ways to "cast" your crystals.

There are many purchasable grid boards, astrological boards, and other "tools" to support casting.

Here is a secret: *You can create a casting map of your choosing* through imagination and intent. Why limit yourself to purchased premade tools, if you can use your intention to create the perfect tool.

Let's say you want to do a 3 stone reading. Each position can refer to whatever you choose.

Examples:

- Past; Present; Future.
- Mind; Body; Spirit.
- Opportunity; Challenge; Outcome
- Jim, Harry or Paul ;o)

Directions:

Simply pull 3 or more crystals that represent "Past, Present or Future".

Sample Divination:
- For Past, I chose Shiva Lingham
- For Present, I chose Citrine
- For Future, I chose Sodalite

In trusting my process, I perceive everything I can at the time of the reading:

"Gina, your crystal representing the Past is a shiva lingham. These stones are often used by healers to cut cords between the client and old toxic relationships. If you feel that you still have unhealthy connections with energies from former relationships, these energies may be influencing you at this time in current relationships with others or self."

"The crystal representing the Present is citrine. The beauty of this crystal is that it is reputed to be a crystal clearer and one of a handful of crystals that don't need periodic clearing. A citrine in this position confirms the presence of unhealthy energetic ties. The good news is that Citrine's energy is here to help! If you don't already have

one, secure a citrine to carry with you. Think of the energies you are aware are from past relationships that you are ready to release. Blow your intention into your stone and allow it to be your reminder that you no longer need hold onto that energy. The color of this stone is in alignment with the 3rd chakra, which represents personal power and ideas we can now re-evaluate based on new information."

"Finally, your Future stone is a sodalite. This blue color is in alignment with the throat chakra. Many people know this chakra to do with communication. It also has to do with choices. You will have opportunities to recommit to leaving those older energies/beliefs behind, while choosing what new energies/beliefs will occupy that space."

As you can see from this quick sample reading, it provides more than "yes" or "no".

In fact, it offers you, the reader, the opportunity to provide real substance for your querant while giving them the task of taking responsibility for their own healing and growth.
As a client *and a reader*, I prefer this method.

The final method offered in Lesson 17 is by far my favorite!

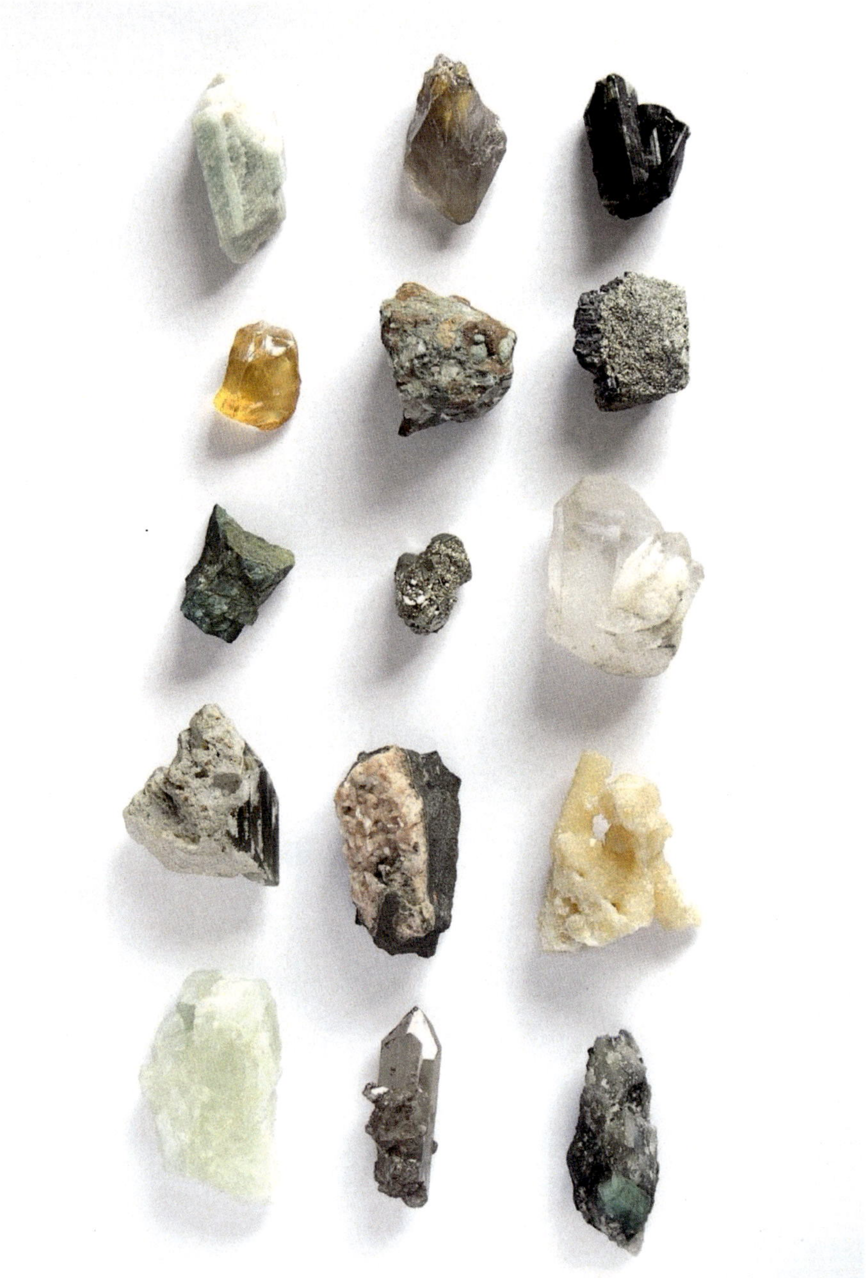

Lesson 17

In Depth Crystal Reading

Today, we'll explore a full-on, in – depth crystal reading that could last between 30 minutes to an hour.

For this, seven crystals are pulled and placed on your Chakra Body Map which acts as your support tool. A color "in body" Chakra Body Map is provided (OR, you may already have an awareness of what color refers to which chakra. If that is the case, you do not need the Chakra Body Map)

I suggest you initially follow these basic instructions before making it your own. They are very simple – but don't let that fool you! You will get profound insight with from this type of reading.

Directions:

- You (or your) client start by blindly grabbing 7 individual crystals from the bag or box.

- Place the first crystal at the root chakra, of the Crystal Body Map, the second on the 2nd chakra (etc.) until you have a crystal on each chakra.

- If the first crystal matches the color of the root chakra, that's "good" and you can talk about why.

- If the color of the crystal DOES NOT match the corresponding energy center, talk about what that might mean based on the color of the stone, anything you may already know about the stone and the specific chakra it relates to. A non-matching color doesn't necessarily make it "bad". Use your intuition to determine the meaning.

The following page contains a sample self-reading. I performed this reading as if I, The Reader was sitting across from myself as The Client.

This dissociative style allowed me to step out of my "self" as an observer with no attachment to outcome.

Tip: Take a look at the picture. At first glance, you can see that the crystals placed over the chakras are not in "alignment" – providing a really juicy reading and lesson!

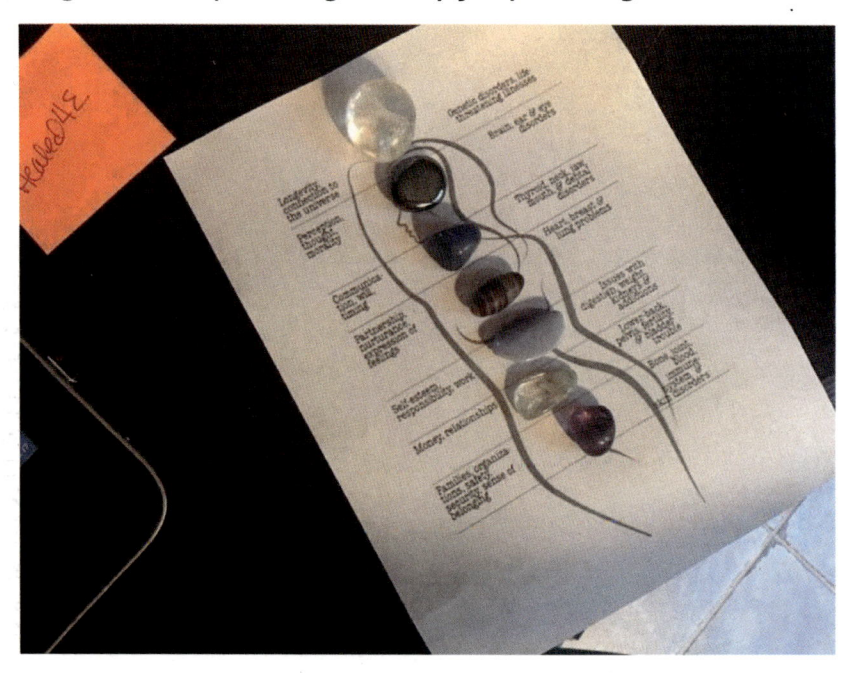

Step 1: I reached into my bag of crystals and selected 7.

Step 2: Using my chart, I placed the first crystal at the first chakra. The crystal is amethyst.

Step 3: I then place the 2nd crystal on the second chakra. The crystal is lithium crystal.

Step 4: 3rd chakra: Blue Lace agate.

Step 5: 4th chakra: Shiva Lingham

Step 6: 5th chakra: Lapis

Step 7: 6th chakra: Hematite

Step 8: 7th chakra: Clear Quartz

The Reading: (Tip: In your practice sessions, speak your reading out loud and record it, as if you are reading someone else.)

"Your first chakra has to do with families or organizations, safety, security and a sense of belonging. In health, it also has to do with blood, immune system and skin disorders.

The amethyst in this position, speaks to the fact that you definitely have a trust in the higher power (since amethyst is the stone for the higher spiritual connections). At the same time, there is not a lot of trust in the physical/earthly realm (as it relates to or organizations or family). There is also a part of you that does not necessarily feel like it "belongs" in some situation you are dealing with now.

You may also be experiencing some immune system challenges that is reflecting on your skin right about now.

Comment: As I do this reading, I'm experiencing a "skin-situation" on my elbow and pinky.

Moving up to your second chakra, you've got something here that speaks to lower back pain.

It may also speak to the fact that you (or someone around you) is experiencing bladder issues.

Just as important, the second chakra has a lot to do with creativity and intimate relationships.

I see you have clarity around what you want to do, but not necessarily how you want to do it.

The lithium Crystal here, tells me that there's a little bit of instability around the subject ..so there's a real need for finding more emotional balance.

Comment: The other day, while heavy lifting, I pulled a muscle in my back. Also, my partner who was laying on her death bed, was also experiencing bladder issues.

Your third chakra has a lot to do with self-esteem, responsibility and work. It also has a lot to do with addictions and digestion and also issues with weight.

You may currently be experiencing the need for more "sweetness in your life".

With blue lace agate here, it talks to me of an opportunity for you to get a little bit more conviction around the direction that you want to take - as it relates to your work.

Comment: Between caring for my partner my son & work, I was overwhelmed.

Moving up to the heart chakra - which reflects partnership, connection, community and healing, physically it has a lot to do with the heart, breast, and lungs.

The Shiva Lingham here has a lot to do with your connection with others... in fact Shiva lingham's are used to remove energetic chords between people... so there is an opportunity for you to remove an energetic cord between yourself and somebody else because the connection right now is not serving you.

Comment: The energetic connection between myself and partner needed to be redefined, so as not have an unhealthy energy exchange.

Now at your throat chakra, we've got a beautiful lapis. It tells me that your fifth chakra (which has to do with communication, truth, will and timing and also has a physical connection with your mouth, thyroid, neck and jaw) - I see these areas of your body being fine. I see these areas of your abilities to be fine. Continue to communicate your truth to those around you so that you can address (speak up) regarding those areas that need support.

Comment: After getting clear on the situation, and communicating the ways I can support my partner, I'm sticking to what I am willing and able to do that honors my spirit.

You're sixth chakra has a lot to do with your ability to "see" things and how you see yourself. It has to do with your perception. It also has to do with thought and it also has a physical relationship with the brain. You may have had some challenges with your eyes lately.

With hematite here, there is a grounding energy - was basically has to do with your connection to the earth. What that tells me is that you're connecting too much with the "3-D reality".

While you certainly have a lot of faith and trust in your safety and security with the divine, (going back to the first chakra/amethyst), there is a lot that you are expecting of yourself, to be able to accomplish on your own.

The hematite is telling me is that you are trusting week too much in the 3-d reality and what YOU must do. Allow the energies and entities at a higher vibrations do the work for you now. Make sure your physical actions support it.

Comment: I have numerous projects in the planning stages, and I'm being advised to petition for and accept other worldly support.

Your seventh/crown chakra has to do with your relationship to the divine and your relationship with your purpose. It has to do with genetic, life-threatening illnesses, but here's the thing: Here you have a clear quartz crystal here!

That means your connection to Source is "crystal clear"; and your connection to your purpose is also "crystal clear".

Your first, fifth and seventh chakras are your primary strengths right now. Your healing and growth opportunities are for the 2nd, 3rd, 4th & 6th chakras.

You have God on your side and power in your lineage."

Do you see how much more insight is given when you layer your chakra awareness to your crystal reading? This is exciting stuff!

Assignment:

- Refer to your Chakra Chart
- Grab your crystals.
- Do a self-reading. Be sure to record/transcribe your reading. Speak as if you are doing the reading for someone else.
- Do a reading for at least 2 other people. Determine where your strengths are.
  This is a great way to get validation and confirmation and support your future clients with additional intuitive information.

Left	Chakra	Right
Longevity, connection to the universe	7	Genetic disorders, life-threatening illness
Perception, thought, morality	6	Brain, ear & eye disorders
Communication, will, timing	5	Thyroid, neck, jaw mouth, & dental disorders
Partnership, nurturance, expression of feelings	4	Heart, breast & lung problems
Self-esteem, responsibility, work	3	Issues with digestion, weight, kidneys & addictions
Money, relationships	2	Lower-back, pelvis, fertility, & bladder trouble
Families, organizations, safety, security, sense of belonging	1	Bone, joint, blood, immune-system & skin disorders

Reading:

Salt lamps

Lesson 18

Each crystal element, inclusive of frequency, crystal system and color – (colors generate specific light frequencies) – offer a very special type of support.

For example, halite (also known as "salt") is the perfect crystal to include in each room in your home that is frequently occupied. It emits negative ions (also known as "positive energy") which is essential to us more now than ever due to cell towers, power lines, and electricity emitted by appliances in our homes.

Dr. Theodore Baroody proved that many different types of alternative healing modalities produce a body reaction that is alkaline-forming.

Many food and other habits increase our level of acidity. (Including meat, alcohol, eggs, refined sugars, white flour and dairy to name a few.)

Crystal Healing helps our bodies get into an alignment with an alkaline-forming body reaction. This increases our voltage – which is good for our immune system.

Crystals trigger our energetic vibrations, bringing about that alkaline-forming body reaction. There are so many things we all do in our everyday lives that bathes us in acid-forming body reactions. Anything that's alkaline-forming, we want.

Dr. Bruce Lipton posed the theory that our cell membranes and DNA scan the environment for relevant vibrational frequencies from different things: hormones, toxins, proteins, light, thoughts, everything which is information. Cell membranes and DNA can evolve and reshape itself accordingly depending on what it needs to be. It can keep energy/information out or let in the information it deems relevant – based resonance.

Remember, we are made of trillions of cells. Each type of cell in our body has a specific frequency range and seeks a vibrational match. In terms of crystal healing, our cells can also be entrained so that it can become a vibrational match to something.

One of the easiest and effective types of crystal healing involves elixirs. **Gem Elixirs** follow 2 specific paths through the physical and subtle bodies:

- The circulatory system/bloodstream:
- The nervous system: Made up of the brain, spinal cord & nerves.

Each system contains quartz-like properties and electromagnetic current. (Blood cells contain more quartz-like properties; the nervous system contains more electromagnetic current.)

An elixir works from the inside out - settling midway between the circulatory and nervous systems – at the heart. Here, an electromagnetic current is created by their polarities.

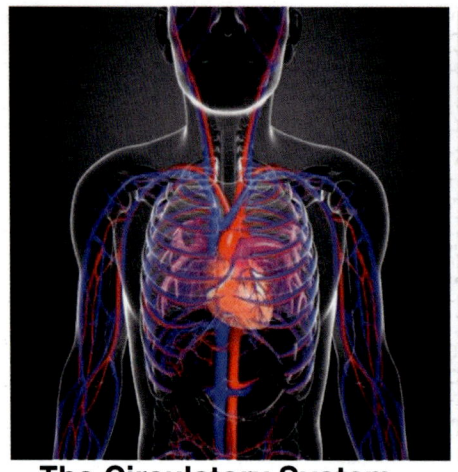

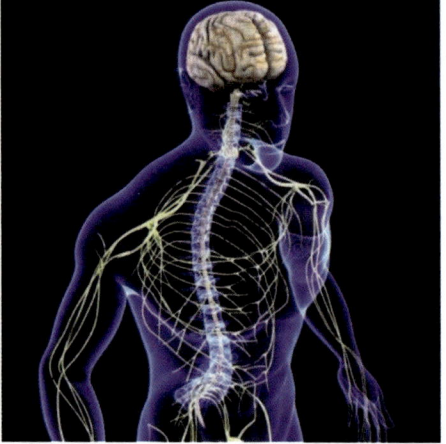

The Circulatory System   **The Nervous System**

*The brain sends messages to the heart telling it to beat. A heart-beat pumps blood and healing energy throughout the body.

These 2 systems move two primary healing energies:

- Life Force Energy (Through the blood)
- Consciousness (Through the nervous system)

Tip: Elixirs can be applied topically.

Creating Gem Elixirs:

1. Cleanse each crystal with soap and water. Be sure there is no dust or dirt.
2. **Take Inventory** and perform **The Tools**.
3. Rub your hands together.
4. Breathe your intention into your crystals.
5. Place them in a glass or jar of purified water.
6. Leave in direct sunlight for 6 – 12 hours.

Try the following "Elixir Taste-Test":

- Create 3 different elixirs using the crystal systems of your choice.
- Taste a regular glass of water.
- Next, taste and compare each of them to the water.
- Finally, compare each of them to each other.
- *Extra Credit*: Use your body as a pendulum to determine which is in your highest and best good to finish drinking!

Lesson 19

Today we explore **Part I of Healing with Crystals**.

Before we move forward, please note: **If you choose to be a professional Crystal Healer, please check your local laws. Many states have laws around "touching" and you may have to be a licensed Massage Therapist. I'd also suggest additional Crystal Healing Training to support and expand your skills.**

Ok...Let's dive in!

In the *laying of stones*, we are addressing the unseen energy bodies around the physical body, and our chakras. Because of the liquid crystalline system in our skin, it is best to place crystals both on the actual skin *and* around the body.

Many healers believe all of energy centers be equally strong, and "balanced". In my work, I have found that our strongest chakras house our strongest gifts – while being the most vulnerable.

Example: *Let's say "Mary" has one bionic eye that can see the past, present, future, microscopic closeness and far distances. Mary's other eye can only see the hand in front of her face.*

One day, Mary wakes up with a sty in her bionic eye. Needless to say, this compromises her. A local healer determines that treatment on her "lazy un-bionic" eye is needed. This healer focuses on building strength of this eye.

Mary goes along with this treatment, until one day, while still stumbling around ('cuz she can't see like she used to) – she hears about **you**.

You know that focusing your work on her strong eye is going to best support her, so she can go back to living her life - complete with her super-powers and perhaps some improved capabilities.

So – you support her wholeness with crystal therapy, focusing on her compromised chakra. Her other chakras are addressed, but you know that her healing opportunity does not include making all of her chakras the same strength.

In this story, the eyes represent the chakras. In my work, I have found that working on the compromised chakra is most beneficial. Most of us are not designed to have all strong chakras. In fact, even those of us who are "shamanic" – (having the talents, gifts and skills of all the chakras) – still tend to lean on a few key chakras.

We are energetically predisposed for success if we honor our natural strengths – but cultural conditioning often supports otherwise. This creates the stress, challenges, and healing opportunities that allopathic medicine thrives on.

Each chakra is typically associated with several stones. You now also have an intimate relationship with the crystal systems. I suggest creating a Crystal Healing Tool-kit that combines the perfect combination of crystal systems and colors.

Tip: I suggest you have both a Crystal Healing Tool-kit and crystals used *specifically* for divination.

I also suggest creating an intake form for your clients – or at the very least, having a chat that would include these questions:

- What healing opportunity brings you here today?
- What chronic health issues have you experienced in your life?

- If you've had surgery, where are your surgery sites?
- Have you experienced any type of abuse? (Self-inflicted or otherwise)
- Do you have any pain now? Where?
- What type of illnesses you have you most often experienced?
- What else do you think I should know?

Questions like these help us discover the <u>common-chakra-denominator.</u>

If for example, "Mary" often experiences chest colds, has had a broken arm, and had a lumpectomy due to breast cancer, we know that her super-powers AND her healing opportunity are in her heart chakra.

When gathering your healing crystals, I suggest communing with each crystal in your healing kit, so that you can identify how each of them will work with you and your clients.

Color is another factor to consider when it comes to understanding the properties of individual stones.

Amethyst, for example, is formed in a wide variety of hues from violet to pink to white. Affiliated with the Violet Flame of Transmutation, it is reputed to support physical, emotional and spiritual alchemy.

However, in some cultures, amethyst is considered "bad-luck", so be sure that your initial conversation with your client includes any beliefs they have around any specific crystals so that their beliefs can support their healing journey

Assignment:

Create an intake form, including the questions above and/or any questions you would like to use or add.

Even if you are only doing this work on friends, family and self, this is a good place to start.

Lesson 20

A Healing Session

This portion will provide the basics for healing via the laying of stones.

A prerequisite for all healing sessions, whether you are working on yourself or others, is that YOU are grounded.

Grounding with crystals is easy, fast and effective. Simply sit with a larger black tourmaline or tiger eye – one between your feet (if sitting in a chair) and one in your left hand. Breath in through your nose and out of your mouth for 7 breaths.

Many healers like to work with their clients on the floor. I prefer a massage table. Choose which is right for you.

An energetic principal that supports healing, manifesting and all sorts of magick, is to first identify and remove any obstacles standing in the way of your desire.

Just like smudging your home with sage, (which is an energetic astringent) then following up with sweetgrass (which invites the energy of joy) – we must initially identify and clear the energetic obstacles that stands between you (or your client) and wholeness.

Once you have created this space, you intentionally petition your intention via your selected crystals.

The Process:

1. **Take Inventory** and perform **The Tools** in your space.
2. Rub your hands together.
3. Breathe your intention into your crystal.
4. Ask your client "What are you ready to release?" Acknowledgement and speaking aloud the energy that stands in their way of wholeness not only sets the stage of healing, but also lets you, as a healer, know what they are ready to release and what they are not.
5. Have your client lay down comfortably, with their eyes closed. Vision disturbs and distracts the inward process.
6. Place a large shungite between their feet.
7. Trace your open hand (facing your client) from the top of their chin to past their feet. This opens their energy field (governing and central meridians – see image) to receive the healing.
8. "Scan" the body (with your hand or a pendulum) to determine areas of opportunity. These areas will "echo" what you've learned in your intake process.
9. Starting at the root chakra, place your stones on each chakra and to the left and right of the body in the vicinity of the chakra. *When working on yourself, place the stones directly on the skin.*

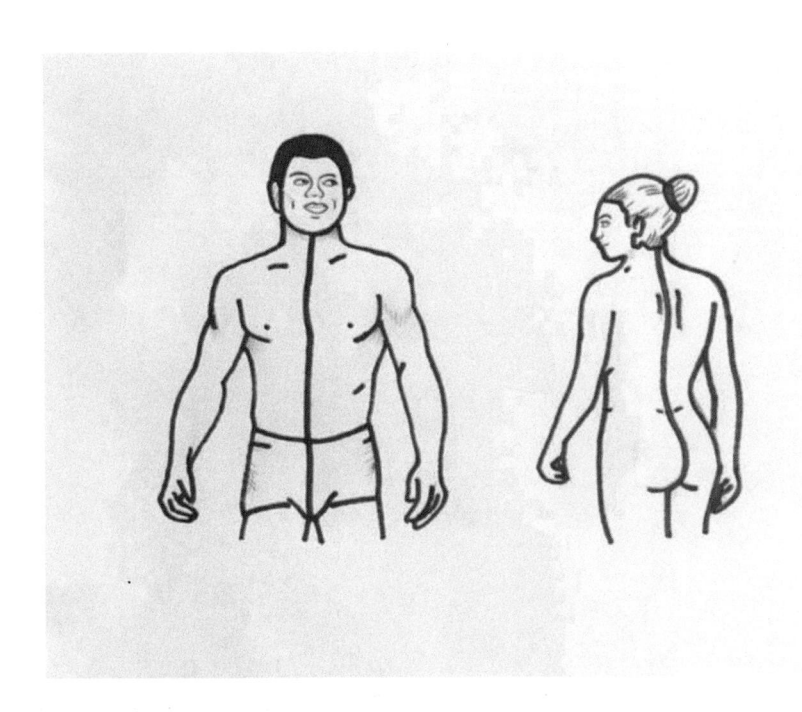

The image above shows the energy line for the Central and Governing meridians.

10. At the compromised chakra, place 4 to 6 crystal points around the chakra stones, pointing out. (see diagram)
11. Place your pendulum over the area until the pendulum stops spinning. (It will spin counterclockwise on most people, but for those who are "Shamanic" it will spin clockwise.
12. Once it stops spinning. Turn the quartz crystal points toward the chakra crystal. Let it sit for 3 to 5 minutes.

13. At the end of the session, remove the crystals from the crown, down to the root.

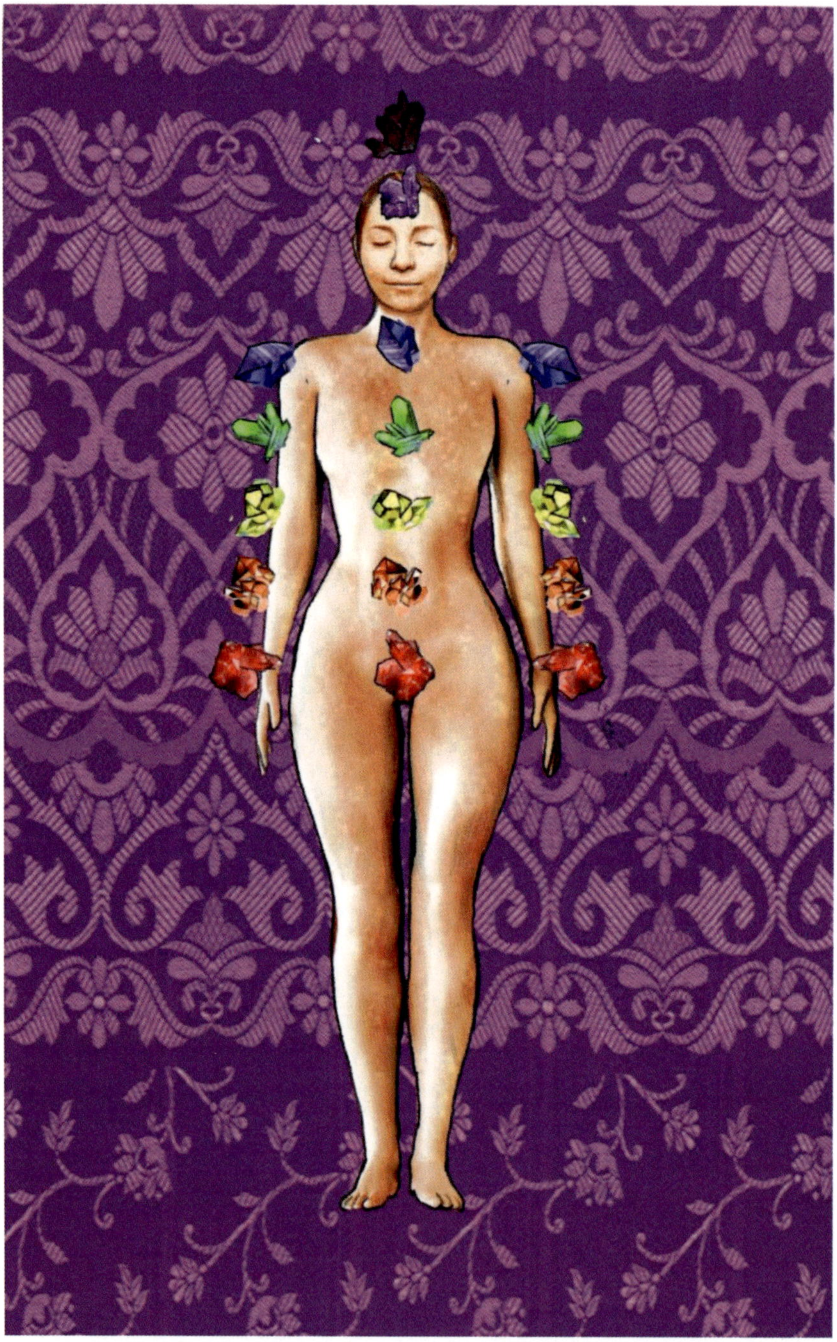

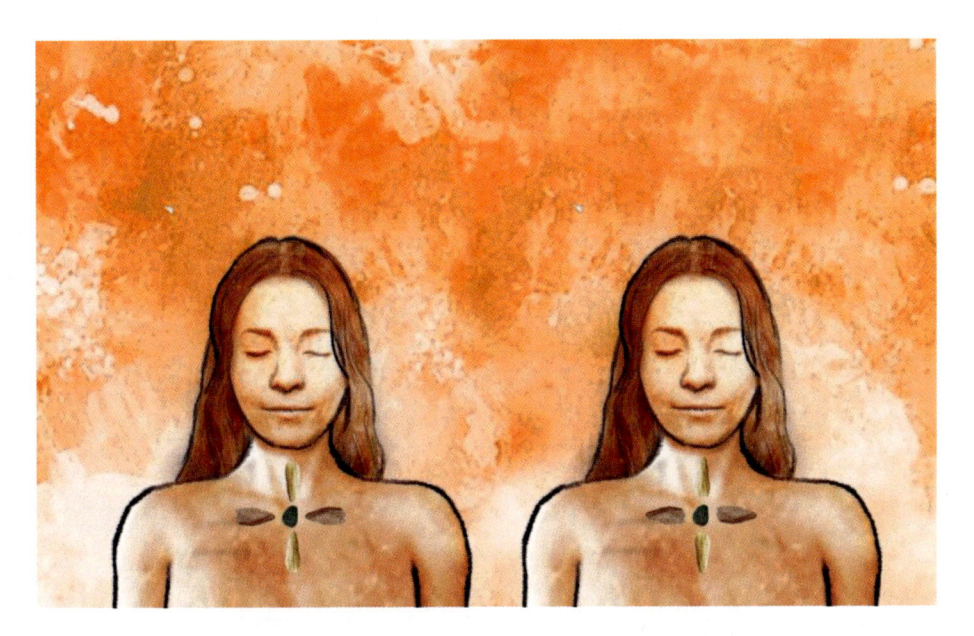

Quartz Stars as referred to in Steps 10-12

14. Final Step: Sweep the aura with your hand (or Selenite wand) from top of head to past the bottom of the feet, which closes the energy field and seals in the healing.

Lesson 21

Congratulations! You have completed 21 lessons and are now officially your own Crystal Authority AND Intuitive...WooooHooo!

Unlike most crystal enthusiasts, you have allowed the intuitive insight gained with each Crystal Communication Session to be your guide. You can now layer this insight with any crystal knowledge you have gained in the past, for a richer and deeper crystal experience.

In addition, you:

- Understand what your unique gifts are.

- Discovered how your chakras support your intuition.

- Activated your Palm Chakras for effective Crystal Communication.

- Discovered a "pre-reading" technique that establishes your baseline so you can easily pick up information - *immediately*.

- Received a Chakra Navigation Tool to help you decipher what your intuition is telling you.

- Communed with each of the 7 crystal systems – THE most often-overlooked component of crystal insight.

- Created your own Crystal Grid - combining sacred geometry, intention, and crystals to achieve your specified outcome.

- Initiated three Crystal Space Clearing methods in your home.

- Explored three variations of Crystal Divination.

- Learned the primary Universal Law that supports wholeness and created an intake form.

- Learned a simple yet effective Crystal Healing Method.

In this final lesson, I offer you an added technique for personal healing AND manifesting - which can also be used for distant healing.

I am also including a unique crystal-perspective which supports how to work with crystals (NOT included in my DailyOM course) that will support you in working with crystals.

BONUS Healing Techniques

You created a personal grid back in Lesson 13 - based on 1 (or all) of your three wishes. This BONUS technique adds a boost of supportive energy to your efforts.

This exercise reminds me of a "poppet", also commonly known as "voodoo-doll". That may sound scary for many and for good reason: The media has made it analogues to a dangerous spiritual weapon.

It may surprise you to learn that "poppets" were originally intended for healing people and relationships. In the spirit of "healing", I offer this support remedy:

What You'll Need:

- A Chakra Body Map
- A headshot of you.
- 4 Shungite Cubes
- Crystals that support your intention

Technique:

1. Gather your cleansed crystals, Chakra Body Map and image.
2. **Take Inventory** and perform **The Tools**.
3. Rub your hands together.
4. Breathe your intention into your crystals.
5. Put your headshot on the body, where the head is.

6. Put your selected crystals on the appropriate chakra AND around the image of the body.
7. Place a shungite cube on each corner of the Chakra Body Map. This will ground and protect your intention while supporting it's coming into being.
8. Leave this grid up for 40 days.

Personal 21 Day Stone Healing Energy Process

Creating your own Stone Healing Energy kit can be an your own empowering tool you can use to heal yourself.

Your bag should include crystals to help clear your:

- Meridians - which are the energy roads carrying your life force. This process will help you remove blockages and adjust your metabolism.

- Chakras: Your 7 primary energy centers - which supply energy to specific organs. The chakras receive and transmit energy/information.

- Aura: A multi layered bio field of protective energy – your aura reflects your chakras. Healthy chakras support a healthy aura. It is through your aura that information (energy) is received and released to your chakras.

- Electrics: as electromagnetic beings our electrics serve as a bridge connecting all your energy systems.

This is a meditative healing process. The meditation uses the help of natural semi-precious stones to balance your energy fields.
Gather 8 stones and a bag to put them in. Each stones color should support each in-body chakra.

Examples:

1. **Red Jasper**: Root Chakra
2. **Carnelian**: Sacral Chakra
3. **Golden Quartz**: Solar Plexus
4. **Green Aventurine**: Heart Chakra
5. **Blue Aventurine**: Throat Chakra
6. **Amethyst**: Third Eye Chakra
7. **Clear Quartz**: Crown Chakra

*Include an **extra Citrine** to keep the stones clear.

Meditation

This treatment requires a 21 day commitment without pause. You may work with or without an intention.
A sample intention is "I invite the loving, healing energy of the Universe to free me of undesirable energy".
Note: You can create a personalized intention that resonates with you.

WARNING: If you skip a day for any reason, *you must start over.* Each day builds upon the next.
You are honoring each internal energy center for period of three days. The energy clearing starts at the root chakra and continues to travel up. You may feel resistance around days seven, eight, or nine. This represents your ego's (third chakra) resistance to change.

Repeat this exercise every three months to stay clear.

The meditation will take between 10 to 20 minutes.

Directions:

1. Stand or lay down. If standing, place your feet and hips with a part.

2. Hold the stones in your left hand and place them over your high heart (slightly above your heart). Gently cover your left hand with your right.

3. Close your eyes, take a few deep breaths in through your nose and out of your mouth while allowing yourself to feel the energy. You may experience your heart pounding that segues into a rocking motion within your body. You may literally feel the energy working its way throughout your body. Some people feel hot. Everyone experiences what they need differently.

4. It is important to allow your body to finish each session so that energy does not get stuck in your body. You may experience little stops and changes in movement during your meditation. You know you are done with your session when you take a giant exhale or sigh.

5. When done take the time to re-ground before doing your normal activities.

After your initial 21 day clearing process, you may want to sleep with your pouch if you're having trouble sleeping. These crystals will now and always resonate with your energy. Treat them with respect as you would a friend.

Unique Crystal Perspective

The Doctrine of Signatures is founded on the theory of "like cures like". It states that herbs that resemble parts of the body can be used to treat those same parts of the body. For example, walnuts are reputed for being good for brain health, while also looking like a brain!

Borrowing from this perspective, we can experience a deeper relationship with crystals.

True Story:

In the summer of 2014, I was exploring the city of Charlotte with my girlfriend. We happened upon a consignment store called "Hidden Treasures" that sold odd things.

We were in the market for the unusual and I had just picked up a "spare change" check from a store where I did readings. We decided to stop in.

This place was jam packed with all kinds of "stuff" – from clothes to furniture, so we split up, each of us being drawn to what "called us".

I stumbled upon a table *full of* crystals.

I grabbed three huge crystals I had never seen before. I immediately decided I had to have them.

I went back to the front of the store for a shopping cart (to grab these huge-ass crystals). I also needed to ask what they were.

When I rolled up to the person at the counter, I asked what they were.

His response?

"Rocks."

That made me smile from the inside out because if there was one thing I knew, it was this: These were more than "rocks".

I then asked the price of them, and he told me he had to call the "consignee" to ask.

I meandered around the store as he did that, and when he found me he said: "The guy" said he would sell me his entire inventory for $350.

Here's the thing: The check I had just picked up was for $350 and there was a table FULL of HUGE ASS crystals. I thought about it for about 3 seconds before I said "ok!"

Fast forward to 2016.

My girlfriend – who I was with when I discovered these crystals - was diagnosed with cancer and died. 90% of the crystals I picked up while I was with her that day are in the shape of a heart.

I gave her a huge black obsidian, that was in the shape of a heart. There was also a large natural rose quartz, large dog tooth crystal and even apopholyte in the shape of a heart!

I stumbled upon this fact while was I was deep in grief. I realized the stones were telling me she loves me and was around me all the time. When she was alive, neither one of us picked up this detail up, but now it is SO obvious to me!

When I refer to **The Doctrine of Signatures,** *like with herbs, it is the visual component* I invite you to consider.

Tip: Ask yourself what my definitions mean to you. (If you disagree with my descriptions, ask yourself what *you* see.)

Examples:

Scepter Crystals: Remind me of the head of a penis. Can be used to direct energy.

Heart shaped crystals: (Reversed) look like breasts. Can be used for physical or emotional matters of the heart.

Clusters often look like miniature cities. Perfect for radiating energy in many directions at the same time.

Lasers look like fingers – perfect for directing energy.

Spheres look like globes – perfect for emanating energy in a room.

Geodes look like caves – perfect for conserving energy.

Next Steps...

Another favorite way I use crystals is to combine them with Intuitive Tarot Readings.

You can either support your *Crystal Divination* by pulling a "next step" card or support your *Intuitive Tarot Reading* by pulling a "next step" crystal.

If you are a tarot enthusiast, this is your formal invitation to explore **The Intuitive Tarot Workbook** or my course **The Art of Intuitive Tarot** on Daily OM. This meaty 21-day course will have you reading like a pro!

Thank you SO much for allowing me to be your guide...I am SO grateful for the opportunity!

May your continued journey bring you bountiful blessings, wisdom and all the support you need to be your most empowered self.

Crystal Communication Session 1

Keep your Intuitive Style in mind with ALL exercises.

When you held your crystal in your right hand with your left hand over it, what did you feel/sense/see after the second *Taking Inventory*?

Which chakra "spoke" to you. (Not to be confused with your dominant chakra, although it may be the same.) Every chakra is related to an area of your body determined by location. Refer to your **Chakra Navigation Tool** if needed.

When you asked yourself: *"If I knew what all of this meant, what would it mean?"* - what answer did you get?

Crystal Communication Session 1a

What did you feel/sense/see after the second Taking Inventory?

Which chakra "spoke" to you. (Not to be confused with your dominant chakra, although it may be the same.) Every chakra is related to an area of your body determined by location.

When you asked yourself: *"If I knew what all of this meant, what would it mean?"* - what answer did you get?

what did you feel/sense/see after Taking Inventory?

Which chakra "spoke" to you. (Not to be confused with your dominant chakra, although it may be the same.) Every chakra is related to an area of your body determined by location. Refer to your **Chakra Navigation Tool** if needed.

When you asked yourself: *"If I knew what all of this meant, what would it mean?"* - what answer did you get?

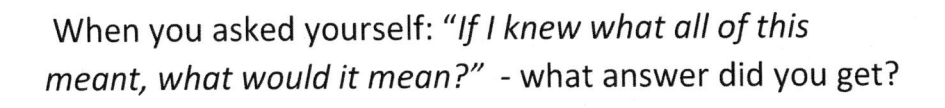

Crystal Communication Session 1b

What did you feel/sense/see after the second Taking Inventory?

Which chakra "spoke" to you. (Not to be confused with your dominant chakra, although it may be the same.) Every chakra is related to an area of your body determined by location.

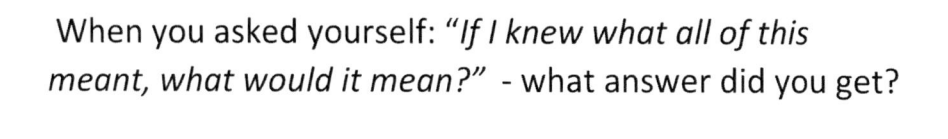

When you asked yourself: *"If I knew what all of this meant, what would it mean?"* - what answer did you get?

what did you feel/sense/see after Taking Inventory?

Which chakra "spoke" to you. (Not to be confused with your dominant chakra, although it may be the same.) Every chakra is related to an area of your body determined by location. Refer to your **Chakra Navigation Tool** if needed.

When you asked yourself: *"If I knew what all of this meant, what would it mean?"* - what answer did you get?

Crystal Communication System Day 2

What information did you intuitively feel/sense/see from your crystal?

1. Which chakra is "speaking" to you and what does it mean?

2. When you spent time in your emotional field, what did you feel that you did not feel when you initially took inventory?

3. *If you knew what the information you received meant, what does it mean?"*

Crystal Communication System Day 2a

What information did you intuitively feel/sense/see from your crystal?

4. Which chakra is "speaking" to you and what does it mean?

5. When you spent time in your emotional field, what did you feel that you did not feel when you initially took inventory?

6. *If you knew what the information you received meant, what does it mean?"*

Crystal Communication System Day 2b

What information did you intuitively feel/sense/see from your crystal?

7. Which chakra is "speaking" to you and what does it mean?

8. When you spent time in your emotional field, what did you feel that you did not feel when you initially took inventory?

9. *If you knew what the information you received meant, what does it mean?"*

Crystal Communication System Day 3

What did you sense?

What thoughts ran through your mind?

When you asked yourself "What else?" what did you get?

Crystal Communication System Day 3a

What did you sense?

What thoughts ran through your mind?

When you asked yourself "What else?" what did you get?

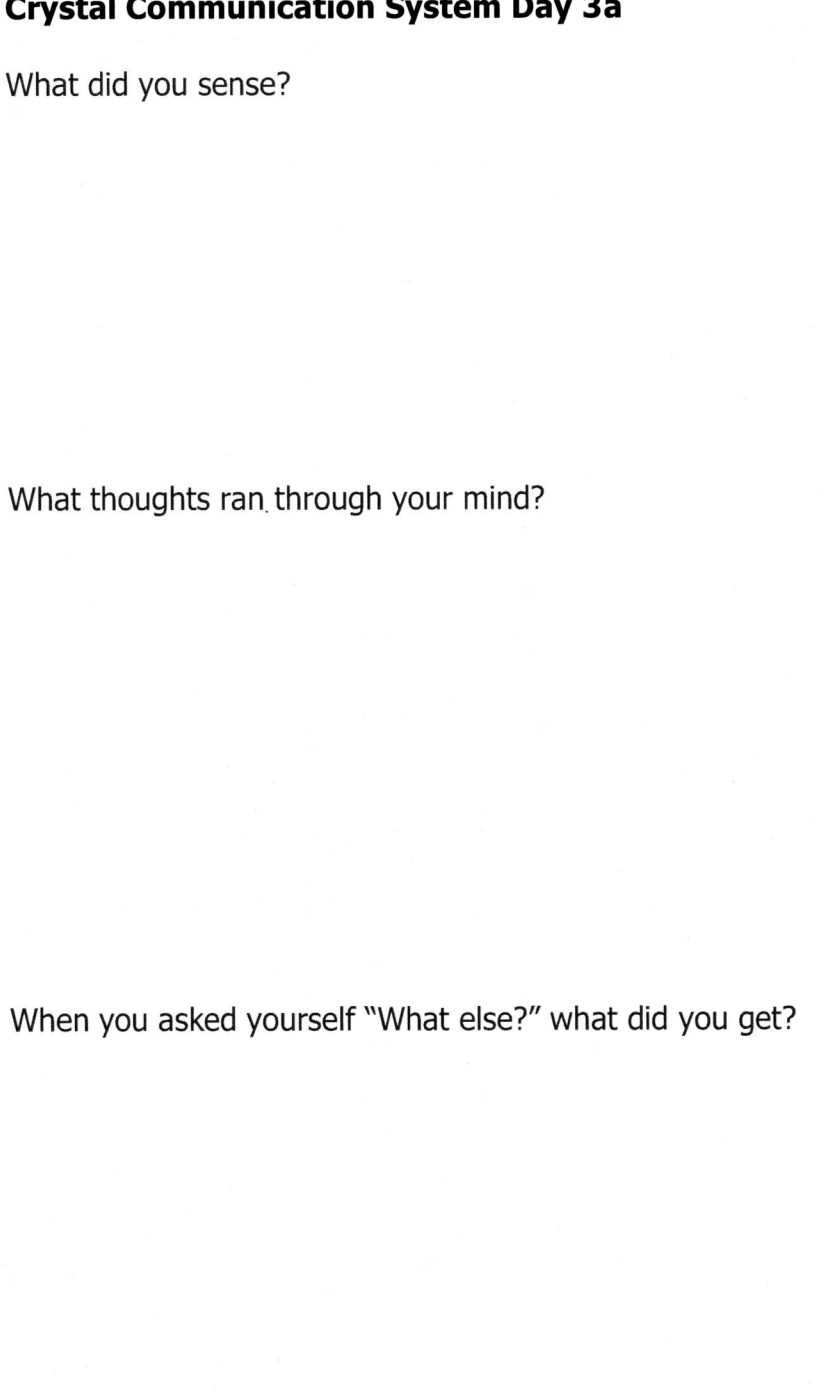

Crystal Communication System Day 3b

What did you sense?

What thoughts ran through your mind?

When you asked yourself "What else?" what did you get?

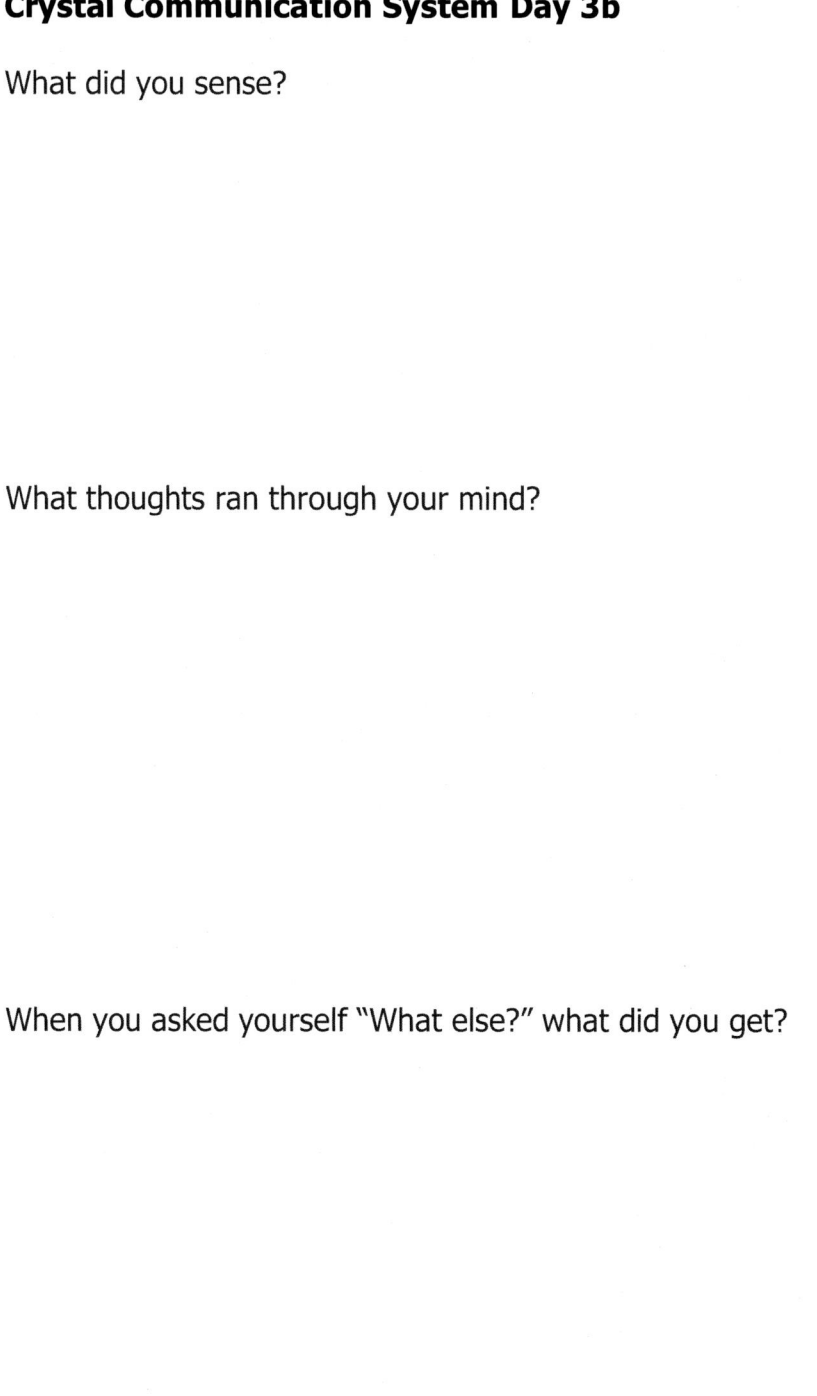

Crystal Communication System Day 4

What do you sense?

What emotions you did notice?

When you inhaled the energy of the crystal, what message traveled to your dominant chakra?

Ask yourself "What else?" when you think you are done.

Crystal Communication System Day 4a

What do you sense?

What emotions you did notice?

When you inhaled the energy of the crystal, what message traveled to your dominant chakra?

Ask yourself "What else?" when you think you are done.

Crystal Communication System Day 4b

What do you sense?

What emotions you did notice?

When you inhaled the energy of the crystal, what message traveled to your dominant chakra?

Ask yourself "What else?" when you think you are done.

Crystal Communication System Day 5

Which energy field or chakra is holding my attention?

Breath in the energy of the crystal, imagining it's message traveling to your dominant chakra. What did it reveal?

"What else?" when you think you are done.

Crystal Communication System Day 5a

Which energy field or chakra is holding my attention?

Breath in the energy of the crystal, imagining it's message traveling to your dominant chakra. What did it reveal?

"What else?" when you think you are done.

Crystal Communication System Day 5b

Which energy field or chakra is holding my attention?

Breath in the energy of the crystal, imagining it's message traveling to your dominant chakra. What did it reveal?

"What else?" when you think you are done.

Crystal Communication System Day 6

What do you sense?
When you spent time in each energy field, what did you feel?
Physically:

Emotionally:

Mentally:

Spiritually:

What new images (or physical, emotional, mental or spiritual energies) do you feel/sense/imagine?

Which energy field or chakra is holding my attention?

What additional information did you get?

Crystal Communication System Day 6a

What do you sense?
When you spent time in each energy field, what did you feel?
Physically:

Emotionally:

Mentally:

Spiritually:

What new images (or physical, emotional, mental or spiritual energies) do you feel/sense/imagine?

Which energy field or chakra is holding my attention?

What additional information did you get?

Crystal Communication System Day 6b

What do you sense?
When you spent time in each energy field, what did you feel?
Physically:

Emotionally:

Mentally:

Spiritually:

What new images (or physical, emotional, mental or spiritual energies) do you feel/sense/imagine?

Which energy field or chakra is holding my attention?

What additional information did you get?

Crystal Communication System Day 7

What do you sense?

What new images (or physical, emotional, mental or spiritual energy) did you sense?

Which energy field or chakra is holding my attention?

What additional information did you access when you inhaled the energy of the crystal?

"What else?"

Crystal Communication System Day 7a

What do you sense?

What new images (or physical, emotional, mental or spiritual energy) did you sense?

Which energy field or chakra is holding my attention?

What additional information did you access when you inhaled the energy of the crystal?

"What else?"

Crystal Communication System Day 7b

What do you sense?

What new images (or physical, emotional, mental or spiritual energy) did you sense?

Which energy field or chakra is holding my attention?

What additional information did you access when you inhaled the energy of the crystal?

"What else?"

Additional Notes:

Additional Notes:

Additional Notes:

Additional Notes:

Additional Notes:

Additional Notes:

Additional Notes:

Additional Notes:

Additional Notes:

Additional Notes:

Additional Notes:

Additional Notes:

Additional Notes:

Additional Notes:

Additional Notes:

Additional Notes:

Additional Notes:

Additional Notes:

Additional Notes:

Additional Notes:

Additional Notes:

Additional Notes:

Made in the USA
Columbia, SC
03 January 2020